STITCH 'N' QUILT

OTHER BOOKS AVAILABLE FROM CHILTON
Robbie Fanning, Series Editor

STITCH 'N' QUILT

Making Accessories for Your Home

KATHLEEN EATON

Chilton Book Company
Radnor, Pennsylvania

Copyright © 1994 by Kathleen Eaton

All Rights Reserved
Published in Radnor, Pennsylvania 19089, by Chilton Book Company

Designed by Anthony Jacobson

Manufactured in the United States of America

Library of Congress Cataloging in Publication Data
Eaton, Kathleen.
    Stitch 'n' quilt : making accessories for your home / Kathleen
Eaton.
        p.   cm.—(Contemporary quilting)
    Includes bibliographical references and index.
    ISBN 0-8019-8483-1
    1. House furnishings.   2. Patchwork   3. Machine sewing.
4. Interior decoration.   I. Title.   II. Series.
TT387.E28 1994   94-15624
746.9—dc20   CIP

1 2   3 4 5 6 7 8 9 0   3 2 1 0 9 8 7 6 5 4

To joyful, creative pursuits
and to the people who love them.
May our passion fill the world
with peace and beauty.

Contents

Foreword

When you were little, were you afraid of falling through a hole to China? It seemed far, far away—exotic, unreachable. But ever since Stewart Brand had the clever idea to use the astronaut's photo of the earth on the cover of his book, *The Whole Earth Catalog,* we've looked at the world differently. Arbitrary national boundaries seem to blur; distances become trivial, what with international phone lines and e-mail; what happens halfway around the world eventually affects us.

One of the things I like about quiltmaking, besides the peacefulness of doing it, is that it's like an international language. You could "speak" it in any country and gather a crowd of like-minded enthusiasts. That's why my favorite project in Kathleen Eaton's new book is the set of place mats based on the flags of the world. I can't think of a better gift for a friend, a better education about the whole earth.

And Kathleen has lots of other good ideas, too, for displaying quilt graphics all over your home. And while you're making them, think about the possibilities of blanketing the world with country-sized quilts.

Robbie Fanning
Series Editor

Acknowledgments

I'd like to thank Chuck, Jessica, Charlie, and David for their patient and loving support while living with the abstract, creative mind of a quilting wife and mother.

Thank you to Michael Boburka for his talented assistance with black-and-white photography.

Thank you to Cindy Moser for her exquisite, talented help with sample-making.

Thank you to all the wonderful people whose comments and suggestions helped to fine-tune this project, especially Nancy Zieman, Diane Dhein, Gail Brown, Ann Best, Maryellen Radloff, Jill Davis, and Katie Nelson.

Thank you, Carol Emmer, for being there.

And very special thanks to the entire staff at Chilton Book Company for all of their help, and for believing in me and giving me an outlet to share my creativity with others. Thank you especially to Robbie Fanning, Susan Clarey, Kathy Conover, Tony Jacobson, Tim Scott, Allison Dodge, Nancy Ellis, Jeanine LaBorne, Karen Miltko, and to all whose desks this book crossed in its various stages and who helped bring it to a successful finish.

Introduction

Stop for a moment to think about the feeling you get when you climb into bed, pull up the covers, and breathe a sigh of contentment in the familiar warmth and comfort that cradles you to sleep each night. A quilt can breathe the same tranquil serenity by its very presence in a room. It makes perfect sense to extend that peaceful influence throughout your home.

Quilted home-decorating ideas can give you that warm serge of contentment each time you step into your home. It says you care about your dwelling place. It's a expression of your individuality.

Before you ever move into a new home or apartment, you arrange and rearrange your furnishings in your mind, to suit your style of living. Even after living in a home for many years, you may find yourself rearranging your household to give it a fresh, new look.

Creating your own quilted home fashions can renew and revitalize your home without the hassle and expense of redecorating. And the best part is you don't have to do it all at once. A simple cornice that can be displayed on an existing curtain rod can add vitality to a room and only takes a few hours to complete. Add some pillows and table toppers, and you've created a new look with very little time and money.

Fabric plays a key role in determining the finished look of your quilted projects. Although calico prints are a natural choice for most quilt projects, you can create formal decorating looks using satins, brocades, velvets, and tapestry. When using these more-expensive fabrics, you may wish to use a lightweight iron-on fabric stabilizer to give body and prevent stretching or fraying of the fabrics while you work with them. You can often find fabric remnants at a substantial discount to make your decorating cost-conscious.

When doing patchwork, it is best to use fabrics that are similar in weight and texture. A combination of prints can add texture without bulk, but always be careful not to use too many different prints. Choose a solid-colored fabric that picks up the colors already in your room, then add prints to coordinated with it. Many wallpaper and furniture companies offer cotton fabrics by the yard to match their prints. This is a great way to get a decorator-look without the high price tag.

Quilting has become a passion for some people; I too, find it therapeutic. I sit under the warmth of fabrics I have chosen to spend time with and feel them gently hug me as I shape the bits and pieces into a finished product. When I am done, perhaps I see that a piece didn't fit exactly as I would have liked or a row of stitching wasn't exactly where it should have been. But this is part of the charm of quiltmaking—giving birth to an individual creation. No two are exactly alike. And I am content to have added a bit of joy and color to the world.

Note to Readers: Although 1/4" seam allowances have become standard for most quilt patterns and projects, most of the projects in this book have an added 3/8" seam allowance. I have found this to be more suitable to projects that do more than just lie on a bed. It allows for added durability and washability. Seams will not easily separate as you work and will not sag or come apart as they hang from a curtain rod for long periods of time. And kids and pets will jump for joy with quilts and duvet covers that have been made with sturdier seam allowances.

The exception to this is the 4" "mini" quilt blocks. I have included a 1/4" seam allowance for all mini blocks, except for the small basket block in Chapter 4—The Bathroom. The small basket block uses a 3/8" seam allowance in order to maintain consistency throughout the project. The smaller, 1/4" seam allowance on the 4" quilt blocks is simply for ease in working with smaller pieces.

STITCH 'N' QUILT

1

Window Wear

Your windows are one of the most important focal points of your dwelling and, therefore, should be impeccably dressed. Windows are a source of sunlight, as well as being our link to the outside world. We look through windows regularly. Shouldn't they be beautifully decorated? And what better treatment could there be than a quilted adornment made with your tender loving care?

Window treatments can be surprisingly easy to make. The patterns in this book have been designed to eliminate exact measuring of the windows and special fittings (with the exception of the Bargello Quilted Cornice, which finishes to the size you need).

The following diagram and glossary will explain some of the terminology used in the various projects.

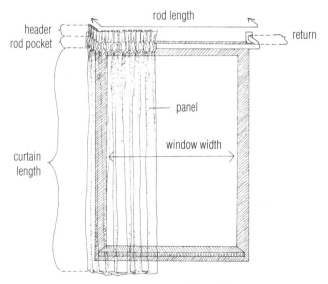

Fig. 1-1

Window Treatment Terms

Backing Fabric: The fabric lining, or that which is on the wrong side of the finished project. This fabric may be visible from the outside. You may wish to choose a rot-resistant lining fabric, such as Roc-Lon's Rain-No-Stain, if your backing fabric will be directly exposed to the sun.

Cornice: A decorative window treatment, usually mounted on a board at the top of your window. The cornices shown in this book are soft treatments using standard curtain rods.

Curtain Width: The total, flat width of the window treatment.

Face Fabric: The fabric (pieced, appliquéd, or whole cloth) that makes up the front of your window treatment (or what you see when standing inside your home). This can be a variety of fabrics, in colors and styles that coordinate with your home furnishings.

Header: The one or two inches of fabric that stand above the curtain rod.

Length: The measurement from the curtain rod to the bottom hem.

Panel: The body of the window treatment or the gathered portion.

Return: The measurement of the short ends of the curtain rod that connect to the wall.

Rod Length: The total length of the curtain or valance rod (including the return to the wall on both sides).

Rod pocket: An extra strip of fabric, at or near the top of the window treatment, in which the curtain rod is inserted.

Window width: The measurement of the width of the glass pane.

There is no strict rule of thumb defining where a rod is to be placed. Generally, it is placed even with the top of the window frame. To "enlarge" a window, or allow for maximum sunlight, you may wish to position the curtain or cornice rod several inches above and wider than the window frame. If extending the rod beyond the width of the window frame, you should measure the rod and not the window width in determining your finished size.

Top Treatments

This section focuses on top treatments, particularly soft cornices and variations, that can be displayed over curtains or blinds, on existing curtain rods.

When choosing which style to make, you should take into consideration the decor of the entire room. Quilted top treatments complement a country or informal setting, although your choice of fabrics can create a variety of decorating styles. Strong, starkly contrasting, solid-colored fabrics can give a patchwork or appliqué pattern a contemporary appeal. Satins, brocades, and velvets give a rich, formal look.

A great source for more information on making shirred curtains to go with your top treatments is *Gail Brown's All-New Instant Interiors.*

Pennsylvania Dutch Soft Cornice

This is a simple soft cornice treatment (Fig. 1-2) which will fit rod lengths from 30" to 44" long (window widths 25"–40"). For rods 40" to 60" long (window width 33"–56"), follow the cutting instructions shown in parentheses.

Fig. 1-2

This appliquéd and quilted design brings a touch of whimsy to your decor. Choose it for a family room or informal living room when made with calicoes or cotton prints. It can also add a wonderful accent to a kitchen or breakfast nook.

The appliqué pattern for this cornice is shown full size, without seam allowances (Fig. 1-3). This pattern can interchange with any number of appliqué patterns. It can also be reduced on a reducing copy machine for decorating smaller items such as pillows, lampshades, place mats, appliance covers, etc. Use your imagination!

You can follow the same general directions to make a whole-cloth quilted cornice in a fabric to match your decor.

Note: This cornice is partially gathered on a curtain rod, so exact sizing is not crucial for a proper fit.

Materials Required

The yardage requirements given are sufficient for either the small or the large cornice.

⅝ yard face fabric (the background of the quilted center)

½ yard backing fabric

½ yard polyester batting

⅝ yard contrasting or coordinating fabric for side panels

¼ yard each assorted fabrics or fabric remnants for appliqué pieces

Align with Fig. 1-3b to complete pattern

Fig. 1-3a

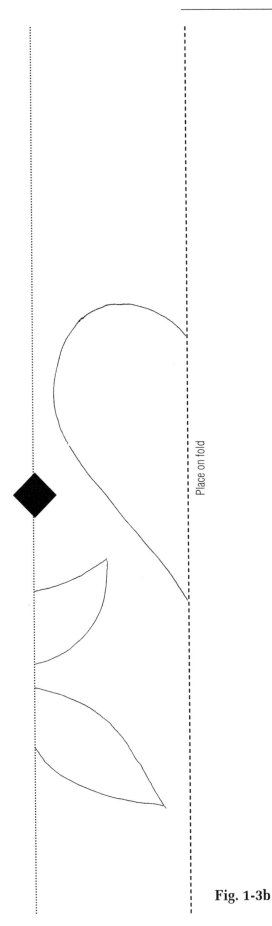

Place on fold

Fig. 1-3b

Paper-backed fusible web (e.g., Wonder-Under) or fusible Pellon if doing machine appliqué

Thread

Tracing or freezer paper for transferring appliqué patterns

Preparation and Construction

1. Transfer the pattern onto another piece of paper, using tracing paper or freezer paper. Freezer paper works well for appliqué projects as it can be pressed, in reverse, *onto* the underside of the fabric, then cut to size.

2. If you plan to appliqué by machine, press paper-backed fusible web or lightweight fusible interfacing to the wrong side of fabrics to be used for the appliqué pieces. Press the freezer paper or draw the pattern on the wrong side of the prepared fabrics. The pattern shown is one-half of the finished design. Place fabrics face sides together, and cut two sets at the same time (cut the heart on a fold). Cut the pattern pieces exactly as shown, without added seam allowances.

If using paper-backed fusible web, peel off the protective backing paper. Arrange the pieces according to Fig. 1-2 of the finished design, centered on a fabric rectangle, 26" × 15" (36" × 15"). Press. If using fusible Pellon, glue or pin the pieces in place.

Using a narrow, closely set zigzag setting, stitch around all edges of the appliqué pieces, using thread colors that closely match or are slightly darker than the fabric pieces. Excellent references for more information on machine appliqué is Harriet Hargrave's book *Mastering Machine Appliqué* or Robbie and Tony Fannings' *The Complete Book of Machine Embroidery*.

3. If you are hand appliquéing, add ¼" all around to the patterns shown, clip the curves, and press under ¼" around all edges. Arrange the pieces as shown in Fig. 1-2 on fabric 26" × 15" (36" × 15"), centering it horizontally. Pin in place, and hand stitch, using a whip stitch.

4. When you have finished appliquéing, cut a piece of backing fabric and a piece of polyester batting equal to the size of the appliquéd face fabric. Place the backing fabric face sides together with the appliquéd fabric, and sew a straight stitch using a ½" seam allowance along the bottom (lower) edge. Turn right sides out and insert the polyester batting. Pin through all layers to hold, and machine or hand quilt around all appliqué pieces. Serge the remaining edges or straight stitch, then finish with a narrow zigzag stitch.

5. Cut a strip from the remaining face fabric, 4" × 26" (4" × 36"). Sew this strip to the top (upper) edge of the quilted center piece, face sides together, using a ½" seam allowance. You may have lost a bit of length and width when quilting, so trim off any excess. Open these pieces to lay flat (Fig. 1-4).

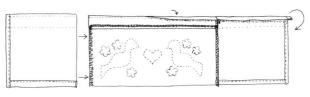

Fig. 1-4

6. Cut two side panels from contrasting or coordinating fabric, 19" x 15" (19" x 22"). Turn one 15" (22") edge under ½" on each panel, then again ½" (to the wrong side of the fabric), and hem with a straight or hand stitch. Press. This is the bottom edge.

7. With face side together and hems lined up evenly at the bottom (lower) edges, sew the side panels on either side of the quilted center piece, including the strip that was sewn to the top of the center panel. Serge or zigzag stitch to prevent fraying. Trim the top edge so the pieces are even all the way across as shown in Fig. 1-4.

8. Turn the outer edges of the side panels to the wrong (back) side using a narrow double fold. Straight stitch to hold. Press.

9. Press ½" along the entire top edge to the wrong side of the fabric. Fold over another 3", or even with the seam used to sew the extra strip to the center quilted panel (Fig. 1-5).

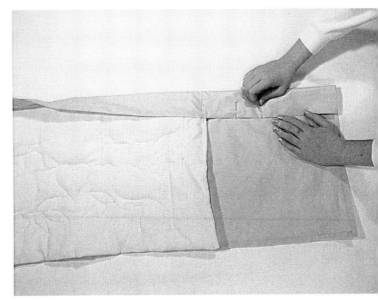

Fig. 1-5

10. Straight stitch parallel to the top edge along the folded edge on the side panels (Fig. 1-6). You may stitch by machine straight through the quilted center panel as well. If you do not like the look of the stitching line on the front, stitch by hand using a running stitch through the backing only, or use fusible tape to press the seam to the quilted back.

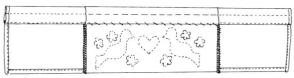

Fig. 1-6

11. Run another row of straight stitches about 1½" to 2" above this one to create the rod pocket, again stitching by hand through only the backing on the center panel.

12. To display this soft cornice, run a standard curtain rod between the double seams that create the rod pocket. Gather the side panels evenly on the rod, and attach the rod to the wall using the hardware provided with it.

Quilt Blocks Cornice

This multipurpose top treatment (color Fig. 6) can be used in a variety of settings. The smaller three-quilt-block version will fit rod lengths from 40" to 50" (window widths 34"–46"). By simply adding another quilt block and a gathered panel section, you can extend the width to fit rods 56" to 70" long (window widths 52"–66"), making this the perfect size for a patio door.

This simple style is made with standard 12" quilt blocks, for which there are hundreds of patterns available in a variety of books. I have included instructions for the quilt block shown here but feel free to change patterns.

Note: This top treatment is partially gathered on a curtain rod, so exact sizing is not crucial for a proper fit.

Since this design uses individual 12" quilt blocks which are quilted before they are sewn together to complete the finished top treatment, it is a perfect take-along project to work on wherever you go.

Materials Required

The yardage listed will work for both small and large sizes.

⅝ yard each of two fabrics (dark and light) for the quilt blocks
¾ yard backing fabric
½ yard fabric for gathered insert panels
¾ yard polyester batting
Thread

Preparation and Construction

1. From the width of both fabrics for the quilt blocks, cut two strips from each for either the smaller or the larger cornice, each strip being 4⅜" wide. Cut these strips into 4⅜" squares. Also from the width of each fabric for the quilt blocks, cut 5½"-wide strips, one for the smaller cornice or two for the larger cornice. Cut these into 5½"

squares. Cut all of the squares in half on a diagonal (Fig. 1-7). You will have more than is actually needed for this project. Use the extras to make a pillow or wall hanging.

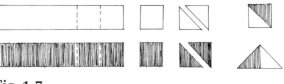

Fig. 1-7

2. Sew the resulting triangles together as shown in Fig. 1-7, using ⅜" seam allowances. Sew triangles along the diagonals on one set; on the other set, sew along the short sides. You will need four of each set for each finished quilt block. Handle the triangular sets carefully—the outside edges are bias and can stretch. Press all seams toward the darker fabric.

3. Continue to sew the blocks together as shown in Figs. 1-8 through 1-10, using ⅜" seam allowances.

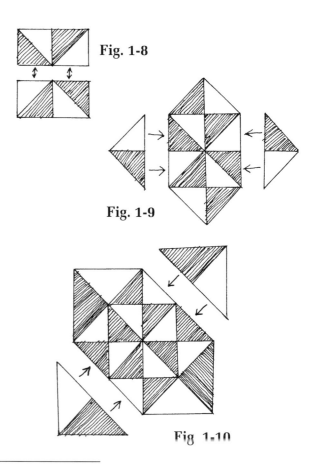

Fig. 1-8

Fig. 1-9

Fig 1-10

4. Cut a 12¾" square of backing fabric and a 12" piece of polyester batting for each quilt block.

5. Place the backing fabric and pieced quilt block face sides together and sew a ⅜" seam along one edge (the bottom edge). Turn face sides out and insert a 12" square of polyester batting between each quilt block and backing.

6. Hand or machine quilt along the seam lines of the patchwork pieces (Fig. 1-11). Serge the edges to close, or sew ⅜" from the edge around the remaining three raw edges.

Fig. 1-11

7. Cut three strips (four for the large cornice), 3" × 12¾", from the remaining backing fabric. Place them face sides together along the top edge of each finished quilt block (the edge opposite the finished seam), and sew a straight seam across the top with a ⅜" seam allowance. Open these and press flat. (Figure 1-12 illustrates this step as well as the next five steps.)

8. Cut two insert panels (three for the large cornice), 16" × 12", from a coordinating fabric. Turn under one 12" edge on each panel ½", then again ½" to the wrong side. Press and stitch with a straight seam. This is the bottom hem.

9. Line up the bottom hem of the insert panels evenly with the lower finished edge of each quilt block, positioning them between the quilt blocks. Place the face side of an insert panel against the face side of a quilt block and serge, or straight stitch the side seam. If straight stitching, finish the edge with a narrow zigzag to prevent fraying and to give it a clean finish. Be sure to include the strip that was added to the top of the quilt blocks. Continue in this manner until all blocks and panels have been sewn in place. Trim the top edge evenly across the entire cornice.

10. Turn the outside edges of the two end quilt blocks narrowly to the back side and straight stitch or hand stitch to hem. You may also finish these edges with bias tape.

11. Turn the upper edge about ½" to the back side. Press. Turn it again about 2" or even with the top edge of the quilt blocks. Pin to hold. This will be the rod pocket.

12. Straight stitch along the lower edge of the rod pocket on the insert panels only, backstitching next to the quilt blocks. You

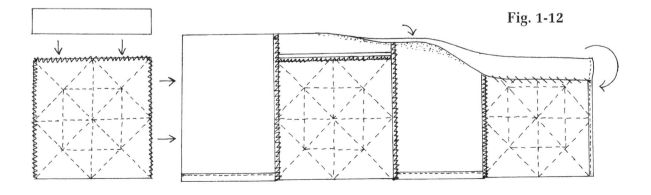

Fig. 1-12

may machine stitch along the entire rod pocket, but you will be machine quilting an extra seam through the quilt blocks. Instead, you can hand sew a whip stitch through the backing only of the quilt blocks, to hold the lower edge of the rod pocket in place. Another quick and easy alternative is to place a narrow strip of fusible web or fabric glue along the lower edge of the rod pocket and press gently (Fig. 1-13).

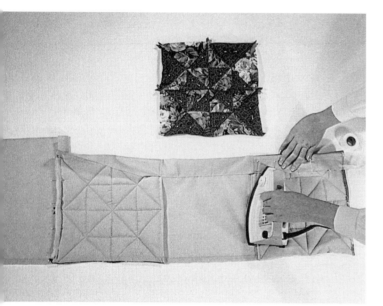

Fig. 1-13

You will not add another row of stitching to this rod pocket, as there is no header above the rod pocket on this style. Therefore, if you will be hanging this top treatment over an existing curtain with a header on it, you may wish to raise the valance rod about 2" above the curtain rod so the curtain header doesn't show.

This cornice can be displayed on any standard curtain rod. Simply gather the insert panels evenly between the quilt blocks to fit your window.

Wonderful Windows

Bargello Pattern Quilted Cornice

This quilted soft cornice takes its design from bargello needlepoint. It is a traditional-looking pattern with a contemporary twist and lends itself to many decorating schemes. Its versatility is accentuated by the unlimited variety of designs which can be created through fabric choice and placement.

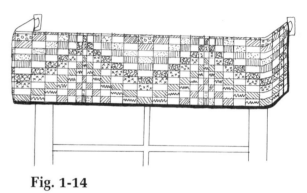

Fig. 1-14

This style is designed to be made to the exact size of your curtain rod, but it is unique in that you will be adding rows from the center to the sides, allowing you to be in complete control of the final finished size.

To determine the finished size, measure the distance between the brackets on which the rod will be hung, and add two times the distance between the rod and the wall (in other words, the total rod length).

Keep in mind that the process of quilting can reduce the overall size of the pieced face. Therefore, you should allow a bit more length and width, which can be trimmed later, if necessary.

Although it looks complicated, this style is among the simplest of soft cornices to make. It utilizes a quick strip-cutting method and quilt-as-you-sew construction for a super-fast finish.

Materials Required

The material listed here will make a cornice up to 52" in finished size. You will need more fabric to increase the size of the cornice (⅛ yard each of 10–12 fabrics will add up to 25" more to the finished face of your cornice).

¼ yard each of 10–12 assorted coordinating fabrics suitable for strip cutting (45" widths)

1 yard backing fabric

1 yard polyester batting (fusible polyester batting [fleece]: optional, but easier to work with)

Thread

Double-fold bias tape (packaged), or extra fabric glue (optional)

Fusible web or fabric glue (optional)

Rotary cutter and mat

Bicycle clips or safety pins (optional)

Preparation and Construction

I use ⅜" seam allowance throughout this project (instead of a standard ¼" that many quilters are accustomed to) to reduce the threat of seams coming apart as you work and to increase the durability of your cornice.

1. Set aside ¼ yard of the backing fabric, to be used later as the rod pocket of the cornice.

2. Cut strips from the coordinating fabrics, 1¾" wide by the width of the fabric (from selvage to selvage. should be 1¾" x 44/45").

3. Using a ⅜" seam allowance, sew the strips together into rows. Repeat the same order of fabric until your set of strips is approximately 16" wide. You will need two sets, 16" wide, that match each other exactly, for a cornice up to 52" wide (total rod length). Press all seam allowances open or toward the darker fabric.

4. Lay one set on top of the other, matching the colors. Using a rotary cutter and clear plastic ruler, trim one end evenly through all seam allowances, trimming as little as possible.

Begin cutting your rows through both layers of sewn strips, starting with a row cut 3¼" wide, and reducing each cut by ¼", until you get to a strip that is 1¼" wide (Fig. 1-15). Reverse this process, omitting the narrowest strip and working your way ¼" larger each time, to 3¼". You should have nine different widths of strips (34 total strips from both sets of rows).

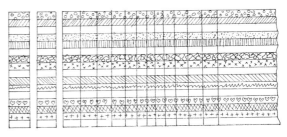

Fig. 1-15

5. Cut and piece your backing fabric and batting so that it is slightly larger (wider and longer) than the planned finished size of your cornice. You do not need to add extra for hems or rod pockets at this point. You may wish to hand baste the batting to the backing to prevent shifting, or use fusible fleece and gently press the backing fabric to it.

6. Starting with the widest (3¼") strip, find the center of the batting/backing, and pin the strip in place from top to bottom.

7. Carefully remove one piece of fabric from the tops of two of the next narrowest strips (3") and sew the piece to the opposite end of each strip (Fig. 1-16).

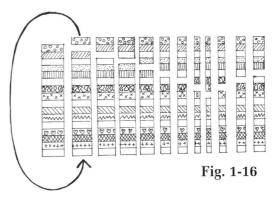

Fig. 1-16

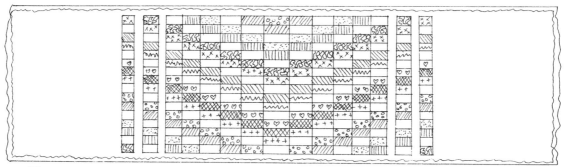

Fig. 1-17

8. Next, remove the top *two* fabrics from the next narrower strips (2¾") and sew them to the opposite ends of each, as before, matching the fabric order. Continue in this manner, removing one extra piece of fabric with each narrower strip, and adding them to the opposite ends (Fig. 1-17). After you have done the narrowest strip (1¼"), reverse the process by increasing the width of the fabrics by ¼" each and removing one *less* piece of fabric, sewing them to the opposite ends, as before, until all the various widths are completed.

Note: All strips of the same (equal) width should match each other when you are done.

9. Pin these strips, one at a time, face sides and raw edges together, to either side of the wide strip which is already pinned in place. All seams should match. Sew along the raw edge with a ⅜" seam allowance. Sew one 3" strip on one side of the wider strip, then do the same to the other side. Sew through all layers, including the backing and batting (Fig. 1-18). You may wish to use bicycle clips or large safety pins to roll the ends of the batting/backing to make it easier to work with.

10. Pin the next narrower strips (2¾"), face sides and raw edges together, to the last strips that were sewn in place. Sew these in place through all layers, as described in Step 9.

11. Continue in this manner until you reach the narrowest strip (1¼"). After the narrowest strip has been sewn in place, reverse the

Fig. 1-18

process. (Do not add another 1¼"-wide strip to the one already sewn in place!)

12. When you get to the widest strip, reverse the process again, and continue until your cornice is the desired width.

13. You may be more comfortable laying out all of the strips in order on a large surface, removing pieces of fabric and re-sewing them to opposite ends, and then sewing these strips together to make a finished pieced top for your cornice before layering it with the batting/backing.

14. If you plan to sew the strips together before quilting them, finish the pieced face of your cornice several inches wider and longer than the planned finished size. Cut a piece of backing fabric and a piece of polyester batting the same size as the pieced face. Sandwich the polyester batting between the face and backing fabric with right sides facing out. Pin or baste through all layers. Hand or machine quilt the seams, vertically, horizontally, or in both directions.

15. Measure the quilted cornice to the size you need and add ½" to the length and 1" to the width to make provisions for seam allowances and the curve of the rod. For example, if you would like it to hang 14" from the top of your rod to the bottom of the cornice, and your rod is 36" wide with a 5" return, trim the cornice to 14½" × 47". Serger or sew a narrow seam allowance all around the quilted piece.

There are two quick and easy ways to finish this cornice:

Method #1

To finish the edges, sew bias tape around the entire cornice, mitering corners, and turning the end under neatly when you reach the starting point.

To make the rod pocket, use purchased (packaged) 2"-wide hem facing (with pre-turned edges) or 3"-wide fabric strips (with raw edges pressed ½" to the wrong side), cut to the length of the cornice. Finish the narrow ends with a narrow double-folded hem. Pin the strip neatly across the wrong side of the top edge of the cornice, even with the edge, or up to 2" below it (Fig. 1-19).

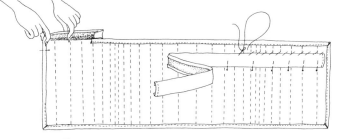

Fig. 1-19

Use fusible web, fabric glue, or hand baste only through the backing to apply it to the cornice.

Method #2

Starting at the upper edge of one side, add bias tape to that side, across the bottom, and up the other side, mitering the corners neatly. Cut the ends of the tape even with the top.

Cut a strip of fabric 3" wide by the width of your cornice plus 2". Turn the narrow ends of this strip ½", then again ½", and sew with a straight seam to hold.

Pin the strip to the top edge of the quilted cornice, face side together, and sew in place with a ½" seam allowance. Ease the strip in place so the ends line up neatly. Open the strip flat and turn the top raw edge of the strip ½" to the wrong side and press to hold (Fig. 1-20).

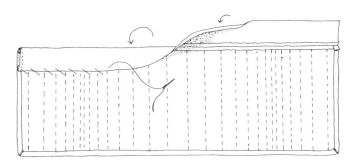

Fig. 1-20

Fold the entire strip to the back side of the cornice and whip stitch by hand along the pressed and folded edge, or apply fusible web or fabric glue to hold. You may topstitch or add bias tape along the upper edge if you desire.

This cornice may be displayed on any standard curtain or valance rod. If using Method #2 to finish it, or if you have not allowed for a header in Method #1, you may wish to raise the valance rod a bit when displaying it over a curtain with a header.

Roman Stripe Cafe Curtain and Valance

These special window treatments are as exciting in a child's room as they are in a kitchen or recreation room. Their simple construction is best suited for use on a smaller window or one on which a shorter window treatment is preferred.

Roman Stripe Curtain

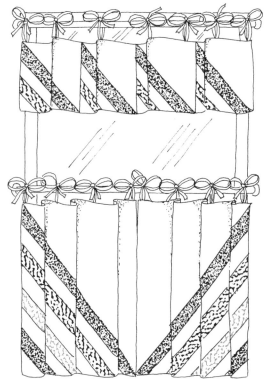

Fig. 1-21

Materials Required

Approximately 2 yards of backing fabric

1 yard of face fabric

¼ yard of 5–6 assorted fabrics (for the stripes)

1 yard each of 5–6 assorted ½"- to ¾"-wide ribbons

Thread

Large paper for pattern making

Polyester batting, optional

Preparation and Construction

1. Measure the desired length of your curtain, from the curtain rod to where you want the curtain to end. For this window treatment, this measurement should be equal to or less than the rod length.

2. From the yard of face fabric, cut a square with sides equal to the measured length of your curtain plus 1". For example, if the measurement from the rod to where you want the curtain to hang is 24", cut a 25" square.

3. Fold the square in half diagonally and cut on the fold. Repeat this process with a square of paper equal to the size of the original square of face fabric, cutting it on a diagonal as well to make two paper patterns equal to the triangles of face fabric.

4. From the assorted fabrics, cut strips 3" wide by the width of the fabric. Line one strip even with the long edge of each paper pattern and pin or paper clip it in place. Cut the strips even with the edges of the patterns (Fig. 1-22).

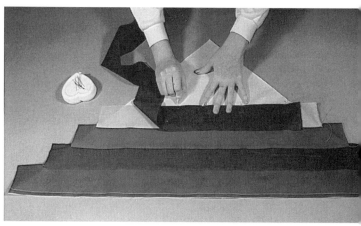

Fig. 1-22

5. Lay a different color stripe on these, face sides together, and sew along the inside seam with a ⅜" seam allowance. Sew through the paper as well. The paper acts as a stabilizer and will give you a perfect triangle. Open these stripes and press them flat. Trim as before to the size of the pattern.

6. Continue in this manner, working toward the corner. When your have completed the triangle, tear away the paper and pin the face side of the striped triangles to the face side of the solid triangle on the longest edge. Sew these together to complete one square. Press. Repeat process for the second square.

7. Cut two squares of backing fabric equal to the size of the finished face squares. Lay the two pieced squares facing you as they will hang on the window. Place the backing on top of these and pin the two sides and the bottom edge. Using a ⅜" seam allowance, sew the backing to the face along the pinned edges.

Clip the corners, turn right sides out, and press. At this point, if you wish, you may insert polyester batting cut to the size of the finished square.

8. Turn the raw edges at the top of your curtain ⅜" to the inside. Cut the ribbon into ½-yard lengths, fold in half lengthwise, and insert the folded edge evenly along this edge, approximately every 4–5". To close, topstitch about ¼" from the edge.

9. Machine topstitch or quilt along all seam lines to finish.

To display this curtain, loosely tie the ribbons at the top edge around the cafe rod, adjusting them for a proper fit. To insure even hanging, you may wish to machine tack matching ribbons 3" above the finished edge of the curtain, tying them in a bow above the tack. Insert the curtain rod through the ribbons, between the bow and the upper finished edge of the curtain.

Roman Stripe Cafe Valance

Materials Required

Yardage given will fit windows up to 40" wide.

¾ yard backing fabric

⅜ yard face fabric

⅛ yard each of 5–6 assorted fabric for stripes (if you are making both the curtain and the valance, there is enough material in the curtain yardage requirements for both)

1½ yards each of 5–6 assorted ½"- to ¾"-wide ribbons

Thread

Paper for pattern making

Polyester batting, optional

Preparation and Construction

1. Cut two 13¼" squares from the face fabric. Fold them diagonally and cut on the fold to create four equal triangles. Cut four paper patterns the same sizes as these triangles.

2. Using the assorted fabrics or the strips leftover from the cafe curtain, cut strips 3" wide by the width of the fabric. Follow Steps 4–6 for the Roman Stripe Cafe Curtain for directions on completing these blocks.

3. When you have completed four squares, place them side by side as you wish them to be displayed, and sew them together with a ⅜" seam allowance. Press.

4. Cut backing fabric equal to the size of your finished face. Using 45"-wide fabric, you will have to seam two pieces of backing fabric together, or cut it lengthwise from a 1½ yard piece of fabric. If seaming the fabric, it is best to have the seam exactly in the center of the valance, lined up with a seam on the face.

5. Lay the backing, right sides together, with the face fabric and pin the bottom edge and the two sides. Sew a ⅜" seam allowance along these edges. Clip the corners, turn right sides out, and press.

At this point, if you wish, you may insert polyester batting cut to the size of the finished valance.

6. Turn the remaining raw edge ⅜" to the inside and pin to hold. Cut the ribbon into ½-yard lengths, fold in half lengthwise, and insert the folded edge evenly along this edge approximately every 4–5". To close, topstitch about ¼" from the edge.

7. Machine topstitch or quilt along all seam lines to finish.

Log Cabin Cafe Curtain and Valance

Log Cabin Cafe Curtain

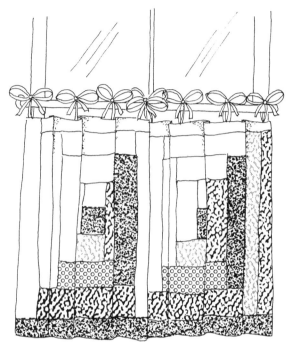

Fig. 1-23

Materials Required

2 yards backing

½ yard each of 6 assorted fabrics (3 light, 3 dark)

1 yard each of 5–6 assorted ½"- to ¾"-wide ribbons

Thread

Large paper for pattern making

Polyester batting, optional

Preparation and Construction

1. Measure the desired length of your curtain, from the curtain rod to where you want the curtain to end. For this window treatment, this measurement should be equal to or less than the rod length.

2. Cut two squares of paper with sides equal to the measured length of your curtain. Fold these squares in half, then in half the opposite way, to find the center of your pattern (Fig. 1-24).

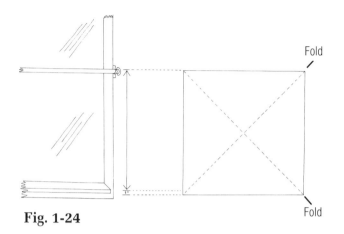

Fig. 1-24

3. From the assorted fabrics, cut strips 3" wide by the width of the fabric (3" × 45").

4. Cut a 3" square of fabric from one of these strips, and pin it exactly on the center of the pattern, with each corner on a diagonal fold of the pattern. (The original log cabin quilt blocks used a shade of red as the center square to represent the fire in the fireplace of the cabin.)

5. Place a light-colored strip of fabric, face sides and raw edges together, on the first square and sew along the narrow edge of the strip, through all layers, using a ⅜" seam allowance. Cut the strip even with the edge of the first square, and open it flat so the fabrics are face sides out.

6. Next, lay another light-colored strip on these pieces and cut it even with the length of the two pieces. Sew on a long edge, through all layers, using ⅜" seam allowances.

7. Use one of the dark fabrics next, and cut and sew it to the next edge of the center block. Continue in a "corkscrew" formation around the center block, adding length to the strips as needed. One-half of the strips should be light colored and one half dark colored, as shown in Fig. 1-25.

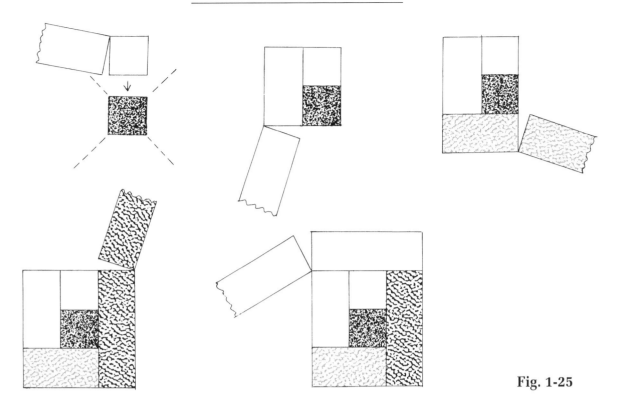

Fig. 1-25

8. When you have finished, trim the last strips equal to the size of the paper pattern, and tear away the paper. Press.

9. Complete your curtain following Steps 7–9 for the Roman Stripe Cafe Curtain.

Log Cabin Valance

Materials Required

¾ yard backing fabric

¼ yard each of 5–6 assorted fabrics

1½ yards each of 5–6 assorted ½"- to ¾"-wide ribbons

Thread

Paper for pattern making

Polyester batting, optional

Preparation and Construction

1. Cut four 13" squares from the paper. Follow Steps 3–7 of the Log Cabin Cafe Curtain to create the squares for the valance.

Continue with Steps 3–7 of the Roman Stripe Valance to complete your Log Cabin Valance.

Quilt Blocks Tiebacks and Trim

These little gems, shown in color Fig. 6, add powerful decorating impact with a minimum amount of exertion. Directions are given for adding quilted trim to existing curtains and valances to renew and revitalize boring decor. And be sure to check out other sections of *Stitch 'n' Quilt* for additional uses of tiny quilt blocks, and more patterns.

These mini quilt blocks finish to a 4" square. You will need approximately nine mini quilt blocks per running yard of finished trim. Measure the flat width or length of your curtain, or determine the desired finished length of your tiebacks, and divide by 4 to determine the approximate number of quilt blocks needed for your project.

Materials Required

⅛ yard each of 3–4 fabrics for each yard of finished 4"-wide tiebacks or trim, plus ⅛ yard of a backing fabric

4½" strips of lightweight polyester batting, the length of your project

Thread

Paper-backed fusible web or fusible Pellon
for appliqué patterns

Tracing or freezer paper for transferring patterns

Small rings for tiebacks

Preparation and Construction

1. Trace or copy the patterns (Figs. 1-26 to 1-29) for the various mini quilt blocks onto paper. Freezer paper works well, especially for appliqué designs, as it can be pressed, in reverse, onto the wrong side of fabrics before cutting out the shapes, then removes cleanly.

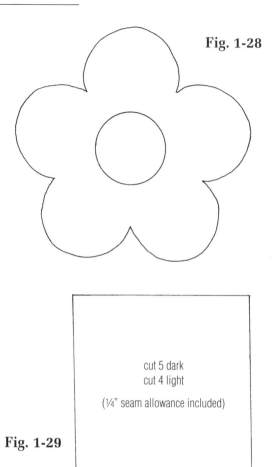

Fig. 1-28

cut 5 dark
cut 4 light

(¼" seam allowance included)

Fig. 1-29

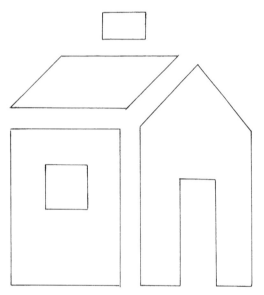

Fig. 1-26

2. For patterns to be machine-appliquéd, press paper-backed fusible web or fusible Pellon to the wrong side of fabrics to be used.

3. Cut out the necessary pieces as directed with each pattern. Sew the patchwork blocks together as shown in Fig. 1-30.

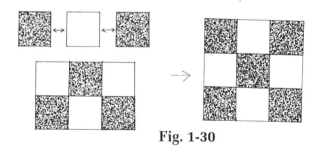

Fig. 1-30

Fig. 1-27

4. For machine appliqué, press or glue the pieces in place on 4½" squares, and satin stitch around the edges with a narrow, close zigzag setting.

5. When the blocks are finished, sew them together in rows (side by side for tiebacks and horizontal trim, top to bottom for vertical trim). Press.

6. Cut and seam backing fabric equal to the size of your finished trim or tiebacks.

To Finish the Tiebacks

1. Lay the pieced face of the tiebacks on top of the backing fabric, right sides together.

2. Cut a strip of polyester batting equal to these and place it on top.

3. Sew down, through all layers, both long sides and one narrow side with a ¼" seam allowance. Trim the seams and clip the corners.

4. Turn right sides out, and press gently.

5. Turn the open edge ¼" to the inside and topstitch or whip stitch by hand to close. Hand or machine quilt along seam lines.

6. Add small plastic rings or fabric loops to *each corner* of one of the long sides of each tieback.

To hang, loop these rings on a nail or hook in the wall next to the edge of your curtain.

To Finish the Trim

For *vertical trim* on a ready-made curtain, sew the finished quilt blocks together, top to bottom. The length of your quilt blocks trim should be the same or slightly longer that the measurement from the top of the curtain header to the bottom edge of the curtain. For more information on making your own curtains to which this trim may be added, see *Gail Brown's All New Instant Interiors*.

1. Cut a 1"–2" strip on the curtain from the sides to be trimmed. On the curtain, remove 8"–10" of stitching from the hem and rod pocket seams on this cut edge to open them a bit.

2. Cut and seam backing fabric to equal the size of the pieced face of your quilt blocks

trim. Place the backing and pieced face, right sides together, and sew with a ¼" seam allowance down the long side that will be opposite the side that attaches to the curtain. Turn right sides out and press.

3. Cut lightweight polyester batting to fit inside this long strip, place it between the layers, and pin to hold. Hand or machine quilt along all seam lines and around appliqués.

4. Serge or sew a ¼" seam allowance along all remaining raw edges.

5. Cut two strips of a coordinating fabric, 4½" wide. One will be equal to the length from the top of the header to the bottom of the rod pocket, with a bit extra to provide seam allowances at top and bottom. One will be equal to the length of the hem at the bottom edge.

6. Sew a narrow double-folded hem on the edge of each strip that will be the outer edge of the curtain. Attach these strips to the top and bottom of the curtain trim to extend their length and allow for the fold-overs to the back side of the curtain (Fig. 1-31).

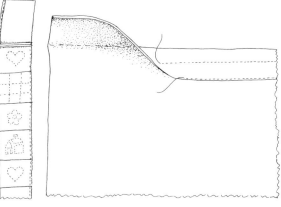

Fig. 1-31

7. Pin the trim to the cut edge of the curtain, face sides and raw edges together. Serge or straight stitch along the long edge. If straight stitching, finish with a zigzag stitch to prevent fraying.

8. Clip off any extra from the added strips at the top and bottom ends of the quilt block trim. Open the trim away from the curtain and press gently.

9. Re-fold the hem and rod pocket seams to the original folds, including the added strips on the quilt block trim. Re-stitch the seams through the quilt trim to the edge of the curtain, or hand stitch only through the backing of the quilt trim to eliminate stitch lines on the front of your quilt trim.

For *horizontal trim* on a ready-made curtain or valance, sew the finished quilt blocks together, side to side, finishing the strip several inches wider than the finished flat width of the curtain or valance.

1. Follow Steps 2–4 for sewing on a vertical trim.

2. Cut 4" from the edge of the curtain or valance to be trimmed. If the hem is wider than 4", remove the stitch lines and remaining strip of hem after cutting. Place the quilt trim right sides and raw edges together on the curtain or valance with a few extra inches of trim on each side. Serge or sew in place using a ¼" seam allowance. Finish with a narrow zigzag stitch if sewing with a straight seam.

3. Turn the sides of the quilt trim that are longer on each end to the wrong side, lining up the folds evenly with the sides of the curtain or valance, and machine or hand stitch to hold the side hem in place. If the ends are quite a bit longer than the sides of the curtain or valance, you may trim some off.

No-Sew Crazy Quilt Cornice and Tiebacks

Here is a quick and easy idea to use up fabric scraps or remnants and bits of trim. Although it's not really a quilt, you will love the elegant Victorian quilted look that it creates.

Crazy Quilt Cornice

Materials Required

Heavyweight cotton duck or light-colored heavyweight denim equal to the intended

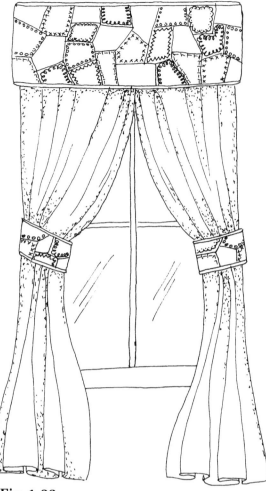

Fig. 1-32

size of the finished cornice (measure length and width)

Packaged wide hem facing or a 3" strip of fabric a bit longer than the width of your cornice, with long edges turned ¼" to the wrong side

Scraps and remnants of satins, velvets, brocades, or your choice of fabrics

Assorted trims and braids

Paper-backed fusible web (heavy duty, for crafting)

Bias tape or braid to go around the entire cornice

Fabric glue or glue gun

Thread, optional

Preparation and Construction

1. Cut the duck or denim fabric to the desired size of your cornice (be sure to include the returns plus about an inch to allow for the curve of the rod).

2. Finish the two narrow ends of the hem facing or fabric strip with a double-folded hem, making it about 2" shorter than the width of the cornice.

3. Center it lengthwise about 2" down from the top edge of the wrong side of the cornice. Leaving the narrow ends open, sew or glue in place on both long sides, or use thin strips of fusible web. This is the rod pocket.

4. Press paper-backed fusible web to the wrong sides of your assorted fabrics.

5. Cut crazy pieces (assorted shapes) from these fabrics, remove the paper backing, and arrange them onto the face side of your cornice as you go. Overlay, if necessary, but make sure the edges at least meet.

6. Press these securely in place with a warm iron, being extra careful with delicate fabrics. You may want to test-press fabric if using brocades or velvets. Trim the edges even with the edges of the backing.

7. Using fabric glue or a glue gun, add trims and braid around the edges of the assorted pieces. Glue bias tape or braid around the entire edge of the finished piece as a last step.

This cornice can be placed on a standard curtain rod and looks great with matching tiebacks. For a super-special look, cut the bottom edge of your cornice into a gentle curve or scallop before adding fabrics.

Crazy Quilt Tiebacks

Materials Needed

¼ yard heavyweight cotton duck or light-colored heavyweight denim

Scraps and remnants of assorted fabrics

Assorted trims and braids

Paper-backed fusible web (heavy duty, for crafting)

Bias tape or braid to go around edges of both tiebacks

Fabric glue or glue gun

Preparation and Construction

1. Cut the duck or denim fabric 4½" wide by the desired length of your tiebacks (about 25"–30").

2. Follow Steps 4–7 of the Crazy Quilt Cornice.

3. Attach small loops or rings, or make a small buttonhole at the ends of one of the long sides on each tieback.

To display you tiebacks, place a small hook or nail on the wall just behind the outer edge of the curtain, about half-way between the top and bottom edges of the curtain (or wherever you prefer). Wrap the tieback around the curtain, and hook it to the wall. Adjust the curtain as desired.

2

The Bedroom

Amish Shoo Fly Quilt Blocks

Duvet Cover

Duvet covers originated in Europe as protective casings for a duvet, or down comforter. Today's duvet covers—no longer limited to a strictly functional use—can transform your polyester comforter into a beautiful "faux" quilt. Any patchwork or appliqué unquilted quilt-top can be used.

The basic design shown here uses standard 12" quilt blocks with added borders to equal a 16" block size. Included are directions for the Shoo Fly Quilt Block shown here, although you may use any number of 12" quilt block patterns, adding borders as shown here, or any 16" quilt block pattern with added border strips. The larger side strips that are added to the outside edges of the center pieced portion are generous, allowing them to be trimmed to fit the many variations in comforter sizes.

Remember, when choosing fabrics, that a dark or bold print on your comforter will be noticeable through light colors or light-weight fabrics used on your duvet cover. You may wish to use darker fabrics or high-quality decorator fabrics for the face of your duvet cover to prevent this.

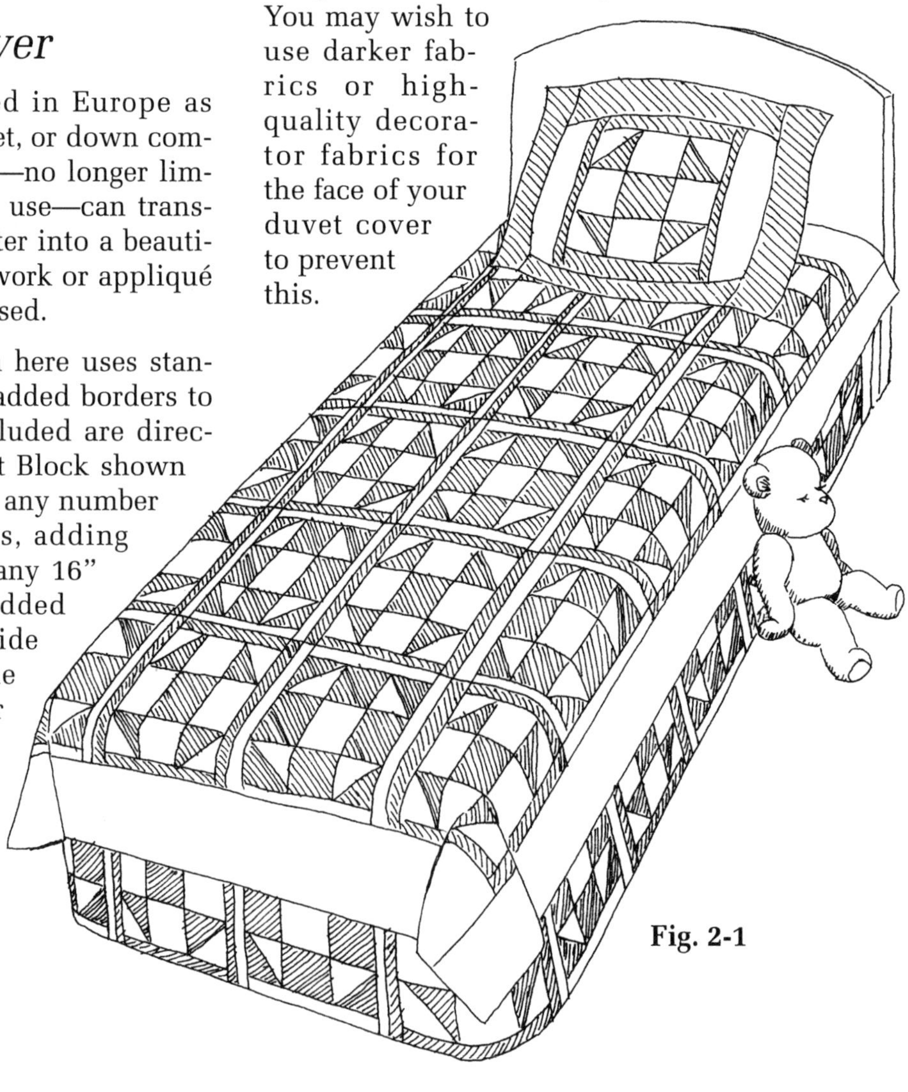

Fig. 2-1

Materials Required

Size	For Pieced Blocks (yards each of two contrasting fabrics)—includes block borders	For Side Strips (use leftovers for pillow backs or extra blocks)	For Backing Fabric Widths		
			44"	90"	108"
Twin—fits approximately 68" × 90"	2⅝ yards each	2¾ yards of one color (I used white)	6 yards	3 yards	3 yards
Full—fits approximately 76" × 90"	2⅝ yards each	2¾ yards of one color (I used white)	6 yards	3 yards	3 yards
Queen—fits approximately 90" × 90"	2⅞ yards each	2¾ yards of one color (I used white)	9 yards	—	3 yards
King—fits approximately 102" × 90"	3 yards each	2¾ yards of one color (I used white)	9 yards	—	3 yards

You will also need matching thread, and ½"–⅝" buttons, or hook-and-loop (Velcro) tabs (approximately 11 for twin size, 12 for full size, 15 for queen size, and 17 for king size).

Preparation and Construction

Measure your comforter for exact size.

Using a purchased flat bed sheet, fabric sheeting, or fabric that has been cut and seamed (one seam line for twin and full, two seam lines for queen and king), cut the duvet cover backing 2" wider and 8" longer than the actual comforter (Figs. 2-2 and 2-3).

Fig. 2-3

A speed-piecing technique will be used to make the Shoo Fly block. Before cutting the individual patchwork pieces for the quilt blocks, measure and cut strips from the 2¾ yards as follows, keeping in mind that these measurements for side strips are generous to allow for variations in comforter sizes.

Twin: 2 strips @ 6" × 66"; 2 strips @ 4" × 94"
Full: 2 strips @ 6" × 66"; 2 strips @ 9" × 94"
Queen: 2 strips @ 6" × 82"; 2 strips @ 6" × 94"
King: 2 strips @ 6" × 98"; 2 strips @ 5" × 94"

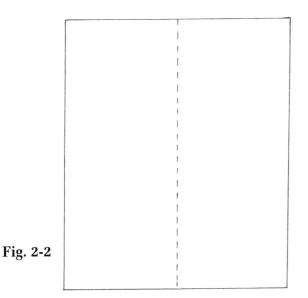

Fig. 2-2

You will also need to cut quilt block border strips from the two face fabrics, 2¾" wide by 60" long. You will need one border strip for each block, as follows:

Twin and Full: 10 strips each fabric
Queen: 13 strips each fabric
King: 15 strips each fabric

One strip may be left over on the queen size, depending on how you choose to lay out your quilt blocks.

Shoo Fly Quilt Block Directions

The main block of this duvet cover pattern is a standard 12" quilt block size. With the added borders, it will fit any pattern requiring a 16" quilt block.

Note: For added durability and washability, I use ⅜" seam allowances throughout this project, instead of the ¼" allowance that is standard in most quilt patterns.

1. Using the two contrasting face fabrics, a rotary cutter, and a clear plastic ruler, cut strips 44/45" long (the width of the fabric) by the following amounts of each fabric:

	4¾" wide	5⅜" wide
Twin	6 strips each	5 strips each
Full	6 strips each	5 strips each
Queen	8 strips each	7 strips each
King	9 strips each	8 strips each

These figures assume you will get nine 4¾" squares per 4¾" strip, and eight 5⅜" squares per 5⅜" strip (Fig. 2-4).

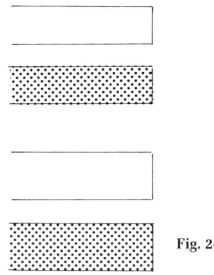

Fig. 2-4

2. Next, cut these strips into 4¾" and 5⅜" squares (Fig. 2-5). You will end up with a few more squares than you actually need. Cut the 5⅜" squares on a diagonal to create triangles (Fig. 2-6).

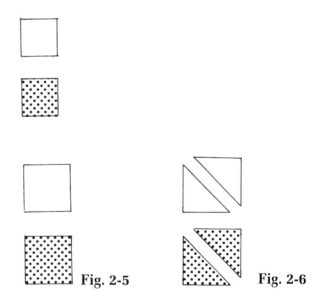

Fig. 2-5   **Fig. 2-6**

3. Using ⅜" seam allowances, sew contrasting triangles together on the longest side to make squares of about 4¾" (Fig. 2-6). Press toward the darker fabric.

4. Arrange the squares for each quilt block as shown in Fig. 2-7, alternating the fabrics for every other quilt block. Sew the squares into strips, and then sew the strips together to complete the block.

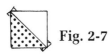

Fig. 2-7

5. Sew the quilt block border strips to each quilt block with a ⅜" seam allowance, sewing them to opposite side of the block first. Cut each strip to size after it has been sewn in place, then sew the remaining opposite sides to the block (Fig. 2-8).

Fig. 2-8

6. Sew the finished blocks together for each size as follows, alternating the blocks as shown in Fig. 2-9.

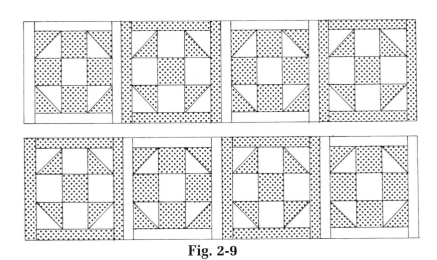

Fig. 2-9

Twin or Full size (20 blocks): 4 blocks across; 5 blocks down
Queen size (25 blocks): 5 blocks across; 5 blocks down
King size (30 blocks): 6 blocks across; 5 blocks down

7. Finish your seams by serging or zigzagging the edges, or use a fray inhibitor, such as Fray-Check. Cutting the pieces with a pinking shears is another method that will prevent the fabric from fraying on the inside of your duvet.

8. Add the side strips as show in Figs. 2-10 and 2-11.

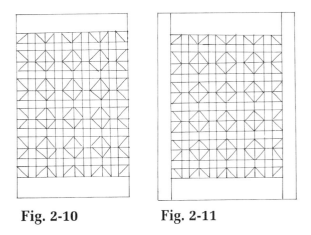

Fig. 2-10   **Fig. 2-11**

For twin and full sizes: Sew the 66"-long strips to the sides with four quilt block, using a ⅜" seam allowance. Trim any excess from the strips after they have been sewn in place. Add the remaining strips to the last two sides, including the top and bottom strips that were sewn on first, again trimming as needed.

For queen size: Sew the 82"-long strips to the top and bottom sides of the quilt blocks, using a ⅜" seam allowance, and trimming any excess from the strips after they have been sewn in place. Sew the remaining longer strips to the last two sides, including the top and bottom strips that were sewn on first, again trimming as needed.

For king size: Sew the 98"-long strips to the sides with six quilt blocks (the top and bottom), using a ⅜" seam allowance, and trimming any excess from the strips after they have been sewn in place. Sew the remaining strips to the last two sides, including the top and bottom strips that were sewn of first, again trimming as needed.

9. Serge or zigzag these seams as before to prevent fraying. Press the entire pieced face.

10. Measure a line 12" from the top edge of the backing and cut along this line for a strip 12" by the width of the backing (Fig. 2-12). Turn under ½" to the wrong side on one long edge on this strip, and again 1½". Sew with a straight stitch along the *first fold* to create a hem. Press. Repeat this process on

Fig. 2-12

the edge of the body of the backing that the strip was cut from.

11. Overlap the hemmed edges of the strip and the body of the backing by 1½" and pin at the side edges to hold, face sides up, with the narrower strip on top.

12. Starting from the center of the overlapped edges and working toward the sides, mark space approximately 6" apart. On the top layer, place buttonholes to fit your button or one side of a hook-and-loop tab, placed on the wrong side. On the lower layer, sew buttons or the other half of the hook-and-loop tab, evenly spaced to match the buttonholes or hook-and-loop tabs. Fasten these to hold the overlap together while you work (Fig. 2-13).

13. Lay the pieced face, right sides together, with the backing on a large flat surface. Center the backing (which should now be 2" longer and wider than your comforter) on the face evenly, and trim from the side strips of the face, if necessary, to equal the size of the backing.

14. Pin the sides and sew them with a ⅜" seam allowance. Serge or zigzag the seams.

Fig. 2-13

15. Unfasten the buttons or Velcro tabs and turn the duvet cover right sides out through this opening (Fig. 2-14). Insert your comforter and re-fasten the closure. You may help hold the corners of your comforter to the inside corners of the duvet cover by using safety pins, snaps, or Velcro tabs. If no fasteners are used, a good shake will put the comforter back in place when needed.

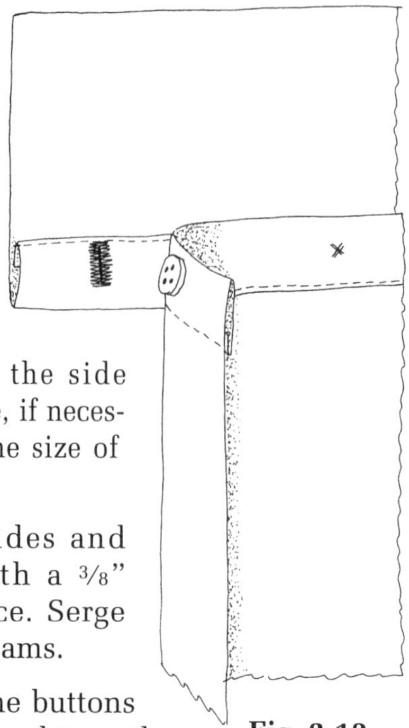

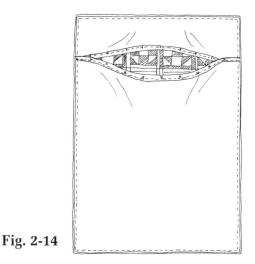

Fig. 2-14

Platform Dust Ruffle

This sleek look gives a contemporary appeal to any bedroom, and is the perfect complement to any Amish quilt or duvet cover (see Fig. 2-1). The pattern for the block shown here is the same as that shown for the duvet cover, and finishes to a 12" square, with 1" border strips added to all sides, resulting in a standard 14"-drop dust ruffle.

Any variety of 12" quilt blocks can be interchanged with this design, with border strips added as described below. If your bed requires a drop longer than 14", see the instructions at the end of the project for simple adjustments. This design is best suited for beds without a footboard and is not recommended for attaching to the backing of a quilt.

Materials Required

Face fabric (44/45" wide): 1⅝ yards each of two fabrics for all sizes

Backing fabric (for back of the quilt blocks): twin/full, 2¼ yards; queen/king, 2¾ yards

A large flat sheet or 90" sheeting, slightly longer and wider than the top of your box spring, for a platform

Thread

Polyester batting (2½ yards @ 45" wide or a queen-size packaged batt will fit all sizes)

Preparation and Construction

Measure the top of your box spring for exact sizing and measure and cut a large flat sheet or sheeting fabric 2" longer and 1" wider than your box spring. Cut a small curve at the corners of the foot end only, beginning 1" before the corner and ending 1" beyond the corner. This is the dust ruffle platform. Hem the top (or "head") edge of the platform by turning it to the wrong side with a double fold and straight stitching to hold.

Before cutting the quilt block pieces for the dust ruffle drop, cut strips from the two face fabrics, 1¾" wide by 56". Each of these

strips will be the border for one block. The total number of quilt strips needed are as follows:

Twin (14 blocks): 7 strips of each fabric
Full (15 blocks): 8 strips of each fabric
Queen (16 blocks): 8 strips of each fabric
King (17 blocks): 9 strips of each fabric

One strip may be leftover on the full and king sizes, depending on how you choose to lay out you quilt blocks.

Quilt Block Directions

1. Using the two contrasting face fabrics, a rotary cutter, and a clear plastic ruler, cut 58"-long strips from the remainder of your face fabrics. Cut the number of strips shown from each fabric.

	Fabric Strips	
	4¾" wide	5⅜" wide
Twin	3 strips	3 strips
Full	4 strips	3 strips
Queen	4 strips	3 strips
King	4 strips	4 strips

These figures assume you will get twelve 4¾" squares from each 58"-long by 4¾"-wide strip, and eleven 5⅜" squares from each 58"-long by 5⅜"-wide strip.

2. Follow Steps 2–5 of the Shoo Fly Quilt Block Directions for a duvet cover. (The border strips for the dust ruffle are narrower than those for the duvet cover.) There will be a few squares leftover, depending on the size you are making.

3. When you have finished sewing the blocks, lay them side by side and sew them together into a long row, alternating blocks.

4. Cut the backing fabric into strips, 14¾" by the width of the fabric. Sew these strips together, selvage to selvage, to make a strip the same size as your pieced blocks.

5. Place these strips face sides together and sew the two narrow sides and the long bottom edge with a ⅜" seam allowance. Turn face sides out and press.

6. Cut polyester batting to equal the size of this finished strip, hand basting pieces together if necessary. Slide the polyester batting between the backing and face of the dust ruffle and safety-pin or hand baste to hold. Hand or machine quilt through all layers, following the seams of the quilt blocks. Baste a narrow seam allowance along the top raw edge.

7. The quilted dust ruffle drop will be slightly longer than the sides and foot of the platform, except for the king-size bed. Mark the center of the foot of the platform and the center of the top raw edge of the dust ruffle drop with a safety pin.

8. Pin the center of the raw edge of the dust ruffle drop, and the center of the foot of the platform together. Continue pinning from the center of the foot towards the corners, and up the sides of the platform. Ease any excess around the corners at the hemmed edge at the head of the platform (Fig. 2-15).

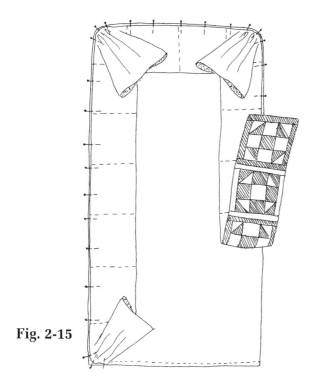

Fig. 2-15

Straight stitch in place with a ⅜" seam allowance.

9. As mentioned earlier, this dust ruffle finishes with a standard 14" drop. If your box spring is taller than 14", measure the difference and cut a strip of matching fabric ¾" wider than the difference between your drop measurement and 14", and slightly longer in total length. With face sides and raw edges together, serge or sew this strip to the upper edge of your quilted dust ruffle drop with a ⅜" seam allowance, turning the narrow sides at either end to the wrong side with a narrow double-folded hem, even with the quilted edge. Attach the upper edge of this strip to the platform as described in Step 8.

Pillow and Sham

Pillows and shams can be easily made with squares and triangles left over from your duvet cover or dust ruffle. These wonderful accents are made from the same 12" center block, converted to a 16" quilt block with added borders, as the one used for the Amish duvet cover.

You will need four 4¾" squares of one fabric, one 4¾" square of another fabric, and two 5¼" squares of each fabric. Cut the 5¼" squares in half diagonally to make four triangles of each color.

Sew contrasting triangles together along the longest side, using a ⅜" seam allowance, to create four more 4¾" squares.

Arrange all squares as shown in Fig. 2-8. Sew the squares into three strips, then sew the strips together to make the block. Press.

Cut two strips of fabric, 2¾" by 12¾", and two strips, 2¾" by 16¾". Sew the shorter strips to opposite sides of the quilt block. Sew the remaining strips to the last two sides.

This square is used as a starting point to complete the following two projects.

To Finish a Pillow

Materials Required

¼ yard each of two face fabrics (or leftover
squares from other projects)

½ yard lining fabric

17" square of polyester batting

½ yard backing fabric

Thread

16"-square pillow form

1. Cut two pieces of backing fabric 10" ×
17". Sew a narrow double-folded hem to the
wrong side on a 17" edge of each piece.

2. Cut a square of lining fabric and a square
of polyester batting, each 17". Layer the
polyester batting between the lining and the
pillow top, with right sides facing out. Pin
the layers to hold them in place and hand or
machine quilt along all seam lines.

3. Overlap the hemmed edges of the backing
pieces about 2" to create a square about 17"
on all sides. Place this, face sides together,
with the quilted face, and pin around all
sides.

4. Sew around all sides with a ⅜" seam
allowance. Trim the seam allowance and
clip the corners. Turn face sides out.

5. Insert a 16" pillow form.

To Finish a Standard Pillow Sham with a Flanged Edge

Materials Required

½ yard each of two face fabric (or leftover
squares from other projects)

¾ yard lining fabric

33" × 27" piece of polyester batting

¾ yard backing fabric

Thread

1. Cut two strips, 3" by 16¾", and two
strips, 6" by 21½". Sew the shorter strips to

the top and bottom of the finished 16" quilt
block. Sew the remaining strips to the next
two sides (Fig. 2-16).

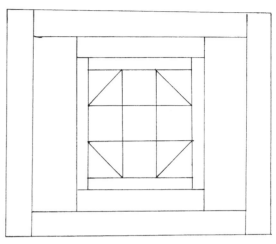

Fig. 2-16

2. Cut two more strips of a contrasting color,
3¾" by 27½", and sew them to the top and
bottom of the sham. Cut two more strips of
the same contrasting fabric, 3¾" by 26½",
and sew these to the sides of the sham. The
last four strips that were sewn on are the
flange.

3. Cut a piece of lining fabric and a piece of
polyester batting, each 33" by 27". Layer the
polyester batting between the lining and the
pillow top, with right sides facing out. Pin
the layers together and hand or machine
quilt along all seam lines.

4. Cut two pieces of backing fabric, 18" ×
27". Sew a narrow double-folded hem to the
wrong side on a 27" edge of each piece.
Overlap the hemmed edges of these pieces
by about 2". Place this, face sides together,
with the quilted face, and pin around all
sides.

5. Sew around all sides with a ⅜" seam
allowance. Trim all seams and corners. Turn
the entire piece right side out through the
overlapped edges, and press the edges gently.

6. Safety pin or hand baste through all layers and carefully stitch through all layers, following the seam line of the last (outer) strips that were sewn to the face (Fig. 2-17). This creates the flange, or border outside of the pillow casing. Remove pins.

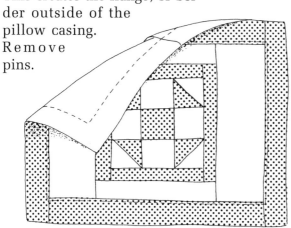

Fig. 2-17

7. Insert a standard bed pillow through the overlapped edges on the back side.

Grandmother's Fan

This popular design (see color Fig. 2) has been around for generations, but has never been so easy to make or had such breathtaking results. The feminine charm of this pattern lends itself to a variety of bedroom decors. It not only makes a beautiful quilt, but also would be a lovely duvet cover.

The center square of the quilt is the same size for all bed sizes, so only one pattern is necessary. Sections of fabric generously added to the center square make this quilt slightly oversized, and the dainty bows are pre-tied and machine tacked in place for a supereasy tied-quilt look. Offray brand ribbon, available in many craft and sewing stores, is completely machine-washable and durable.

Instructions at the end of this chapter will show you how to attach the dust ruffle to the back of your quilt, transforming it to an elegant all-in-one bedspread.

Quilt

Materials Required

Fabric amounts are for all sizes. Do not make yardage substitutions if using wider than 44/45" fabrics. You will want to choose an assortment of large and small prints, and solid-colored fabrics.

¼ yard each of six assorted fabrics for "fan" (fat quarters or 9" strips)

⅞ yard of background fabric (on which your fan will be placed)

⅝ yard for the triangles around the fan

⅓ yard for the narrow border strips around the center square

6 yards of 1"-wide flat or ruffled lace, optional

Face fabric: for twin or full size, 4 yards each; for queen or king size, 6¾ yards each

Backing fabric (see Shoo Fly Blocks Duvet Cover instructions for backing fabric)

Polyester batting large enough to fit your quilt (omit for duvet cover)

Thread

Ribbon for bows, ⅜" or ½" wide: twin, 12 yards; full, 16 yards; queen, 18 yards; king, 18 yards

Bicycle clips

Preparation and Construction

1. Enlarge Fig. 2-18, making one square equal to 1" and draw it onto gridded freezer paper or any large drawing surface. There are three patterns with Fig. 2-18: A (the trapezoidal portion), B (the entire ¼ circle), and C (the area within the dashed line). Using the ¼-yard pieces of assorted fabrics, cut one piece of pattern B and six pieces of pattern A.

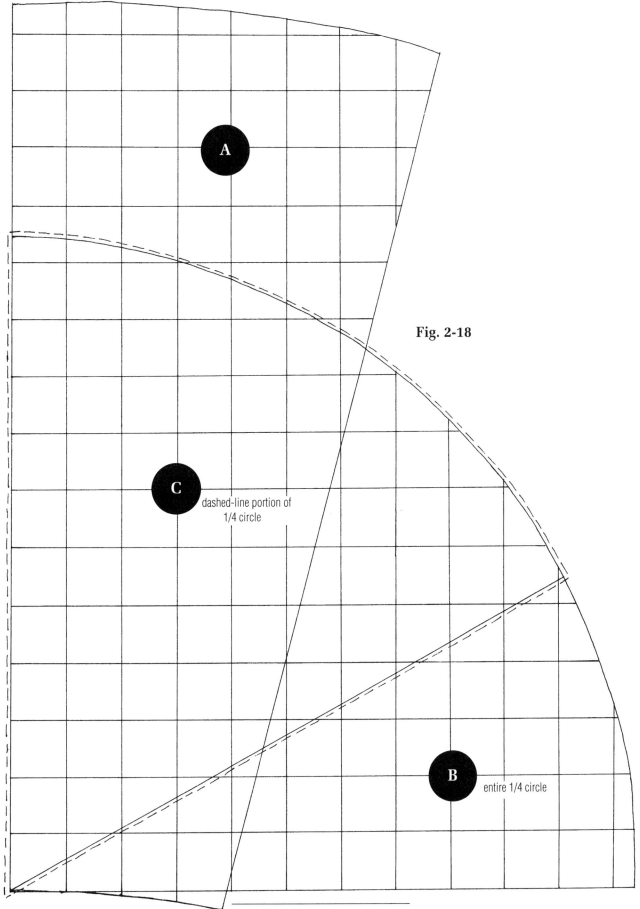

A

Fig. 2-18

C
dashed-line portion of
1/4 circle

B
entire 1/4 circle

2. Sew the fan pieces together, as shown in Fig. 2-19, using ⅜" seam allowances. Run a wide basting stitch about ¼" from the raw edge of the lower (smaller) curve of the fan portion. Mark the center of the curved edge of the solid-colored ¼ circle by folding it in half at the corner. Pin the center of the lower (smaller) curve of the "fan" portion, face sides and raw edges together, to the center of the ¼ circle as shown in Fig. 2-20.

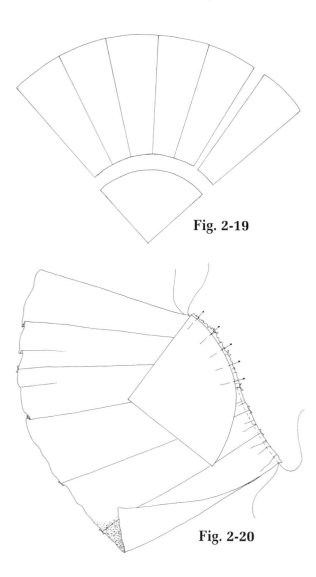

Fig. 2-19

Fig. 2-20

3. Optional: Pin 1"-wide flat or ruffled *lace*, face sides and raw edges together, to the long curved edge opposite the "corner" of the fan. If using flat lace, sew a loose basting stitch along the bottom edge and pull it gently to allow for the curve of the fan before pinning the lace in place. Sew in place with

a ¼" seam allowance. Open the lace flat and press the seam allowance toward the pieced fan on the wrong side.

4. Cut a 28¾" square from the ⅞ yard of background fabric. Place the fan, with edges even, in one corner of the square, pinning the raw edges together.

5. Baste the raw edges together with a ¼" seam allowance. Topstitch "in the ditch" between the lace and the fabric on the curved edge.

6. From the ⅝ yard for triangles around the fan, cut two 21¼" squares. Cut these in half diagonally, to get four matching triangles.

7. Sew the long side of each triangle to each side of the "fan" square, using ⅜" seam allowances.

8. Optional: Sew flat or ruffled lace, face sides and raw edges together, around all sides of this finished square with a ⅜" seam allowance, pinching the lace at the corners before sewing it in place to allow it to lie flat. Position the lace a bit inside the raw edge of the fabric, so it will be sewn on with a narrower seam allowance.

9. Cut four 2½"-wide strips the width (44/45") of the fabric for the narrow border strips around the center square.

10. Pin two of these strips to opposite sides of the square, and sew them in place with a ⅜" seam allowance. Cut off any excess from the strips. In the same way, pin and sew two other strips to the remaining sides of the squares. Press the lace toward the outside edges.

11. From the added yardage for the face of the quilt, cut a piece of fabric 28½" by the width of the fabric, and sew it with a ⅜" seam allowance to the top of the square "fan" section, aligning a 44/45" edge of the fabric to the side of the fan square.

12. Likewise, cut a 22½" section of added fabric, the width of the fabric and sew it to the bottom of the fan square, as before. If these fabric widths are slightly wider than your finished fan square, simply trim the excess evenly across a selvage edge.

13. Side sections will be cut from the remaining fabric as follows:

Twin size: two strips, 14" wide × 93" long

Full size: two strips, 18" wide × 93" long

Queen size: two strips 25" × 93" long

King size: two strips, 31" wide × 93" long

14. Pin the long edges of the side strips to the long edges of the finished center section, and sew them in place with a ⅜" seam allowance. Cut excess from the top or bottom edges as necessary.

15. Fold the entire finished quilt face in half lengthwise and finger press to find a center line from top to bottom, to aide you in measuring for bow placement.

16. With a marking pencil or erasable marking pen and a yardstick, place a small dot on your quilt face at each x shown in Figs. 2-21 to 2-23 for the different sizes. These are the points at which your bows will be placed. I used 10" intervals, indicated by the x in diagrams.

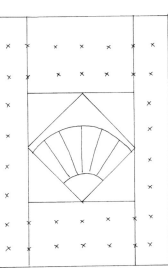

Twin size

Fig. 2-21

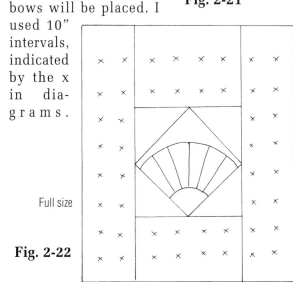

Full size

Fig. 2-22

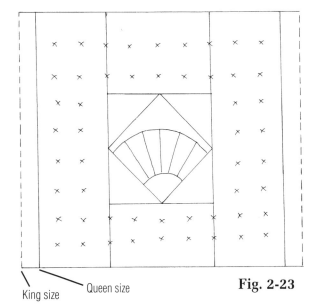

King size   Queen size

Fig. 2-23

Don't worry too much if they don't line up exactly as shown.

17. If using 44/45"-wide fabric for your backing, cut two 93"-long sections for twin and full sizes, and three 93"-long sections for queen and king sizes. Sew these together on the long edges with ⅜" seam allowances. (One seam line for twin and full, two seam lines for queen and king.) (See Figs. 2-2 and 2-3.)

18. Whether you are using seamed fabric, wide sheeting, or a flat sheet, lay the backing on a large flat surface, face side up. Lay the face of your quilt, centered on the backing, face side down. Cut the backing to the size of the face.

19. Lay your polyester batting on top of these pieces, and trim it to the same size. Pin the two long sides and the bottom or foot end through all layers to hold them together. Sew the layers together along the pinned sides with a ⅜" seam allowance, removing pins as you sew. Trim excess from the seam allowance and clip the corners.

20. Turn the entire piece face sides out. Stitch by hand or safety pin at each marking made on the face of the quilt for bow placement. Turn the remaining open edge narrowly to the inside, pinning to hold. Machine topstitch with a straight stitch near the edge.

21. Roll the sides of your quilt and hold them with bicycle clips. Hand or machine quilt, following the seam lines of the center pieced square and fan sections. Include the seam lines of the border strips that were added around the center square, but not the seam lines of the side strips added last.

22. Cut your ribbon into 10" pieces and loosely tie each piece into a bow. You should be able to flatten the knot somewhat.

23. Position the first mark on your quilt directly under the needle of your machine (Fig. 2-24). Take a few stitches, then lift the presser foot and slide a bow on top of the stitches. Stitch back and forth a few times across the knot of the bow to secure it in place. Repeat this process for each mark.

Fig. 2-24

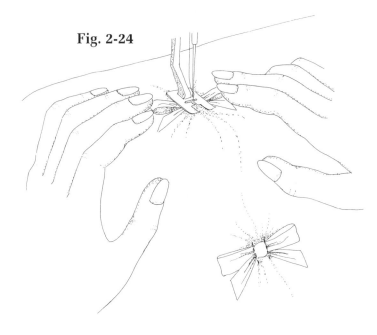

Dust Ruffle

This unique petticoat is made up of quilted fans connected by sections of shirred fabric. It is the perfect complement to the Grandmother's Fan Quilt and creates a "sculptured" base for your bed (color Fig. 2).

Don't be intimidated by its unusual appearance. This dust ruffle is surprisingly easy to make. The same construction used for this dust ruffle can be adapted for use

with any 12" quilt block pattern, as explained later in the instructions.

For a fabulous all-in-one bedspread, check out the instructions for attaching this dust ruffle to the backing of any finished quilt or quilt-in-progress. If you would like to attach your dust ruffle to a quilt backing, read the directions for both the dust ruffle and how to attach it before beginning your project.

Materials Required

Face fabric: ½ yard each of 5–6 assorted fabrics for the quilted fans

Insert panels (gathered section of fabric between the quilted fans): twin, full, and queen sizes, 3¼ yards; king size, 3⅝ yards

Backing and polyester batting: 2 yards for all sizes

Platforms (omit if attaching to a quilt backing): large flat sheet or 90" sheeting slightly longer and wider than the top of your box spring

Thread

Lace, optional: 5–6 yards for all sizes, to be topstitched to quilted fans

Preparation and Construction

1. Transfer the fan quilt pattern pieces to tracing or freezer paper, using the actual sizes shown in Fig. 2-18.

2. You will need the following number of finished fans for each size:

Twin size: 10 regular fans, 2 corner fans
Full size: 11 regular fans, 2 corner fans
Queen size: 13 regular fans, 2 corner fans
King size: 14 regular fans, 2 corner fans

3. Cut the necessary number of pieces according to the following list:

All sizes: cut 2 of B (for use as the corner fans); cut 12 of A (6 for each corner fan)
Twin: cut 10 of C; cut 40 of A (assorted fabrics)

Fig. 1 *"Stained Glass"*
lampshade

Fig. 2

Fig. 2 *Grandmother's Fan quilt, dust ruffle, and pillow sham.* Fig. 3 *Grandmother's Fan pillow sham.* Fig. 4 *Matching window treatment (directions not given).*

Fig. 3

Fig. 4

Fig. 5

Fig. 6

Fig. 5 *Pennsylvania Dutch appliqué lampshade, Hawaiian Quilt table topper, and Quilt Blocks tiebacks and trim.*

Fig. 6 *Quilt Blocks cornice, tiebacks, and trim.*

Fig. 7 *Patchwork quilted one-piece rocker/chair cushion and Hawaiian Quilt coasters.*

Fig. 7

Fig. 8

Fig. 9

Fig. 10

Fig. 8 *Morning Glory chair pad, seat back, and place mats.*

Fig. 9 *Morning Glory appliance covers and oven mitt.*

Fig. 10 *Flags of the World place mats.*

Fig. 11 *Trip Around the World table-cloth.*

Fig. 11

Figs. 12 & 13 *Flower Basket bathroom accessories.*

Fig. 12

Fig. 13

Full: cut 11 of C; cut 44 of A (assorted)
Queen: cut 13 of C; cut 52 of A (assorted)
King: cut 14 of C; cut 56 of A (assorted)

Sew the fans together as shown in Fig. 2-25, using ⅜" seam allowances. ***Note:*** Two of the quilted fans, to be placed at the corners

Fig. 2-25

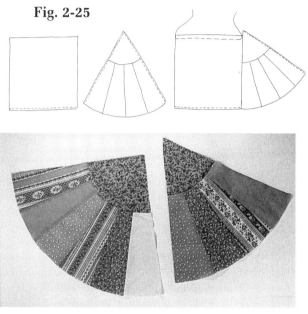

Fig. 2-26

of the foot of your dust ruffle, will be rounder or more "open" than the rest. They are made in the same way as the other fans, but with two extra "fan" pieces. This will accommodate the curve of the corner and provide a balanced look. Read through the instructions carefully for proper positioning.

4. Cut backing fabric and polyester batting equal to the size of each fan, for as many fans as you need.

5. Layer the pieced fan, face sides together, with the backing. Place the polyester batting on these and pin through all layers along the lower curved edge. Sew the layers together along this edge with a ⅜" seam allowance. Trim the seam allowance close to the curve.

6. Turn the fans face side out. Press gently along the curved edges.

7. Sew a narrow (¼") seam allowance along the remaining raw edges to hold them together. Machine or hand quilt following the seam lines on the face of the fan. Trim with lace, topstitched in place, if desired.

8. Cut sections of insert fabric, 15½" long × 22" wide (half the width of the fabric), as follows:

Twin: 13 sections
Full: 14 sections
Queen: 14 sections
King: 15 sections

9. On each piece, turn one 22" edge ½" to the wrong side, then again ½", and sew with a straight seam for a narrow bottom hem. Press.

10. Align the hemmed edge of the insert pieces evenly with the finished curved edge of the fans, face sides and raw edges together (Fig. 2-25). Pin the long straight edges together, alternating plain fabric and quilted fans. For the twin and full sizes, you will start and end with a quilted fan.

11. Determine the position of the corner fans by counting the number of fans from each end of the dust ruffle drop. For the twin and full sizes, the fifth fan from each end will be the corner fan. For queen and king sizes, the sixth fan for each end will be the corner fan. These will be placed at the corner curves of the foot of your platform or at the curves drawn at the foot end of your backing if following the directions for attaching your dust ruffle to the quilt backing. (Fig. 2-27)

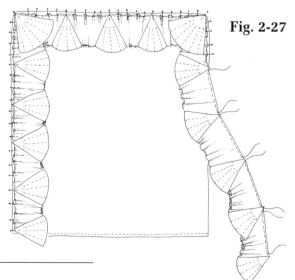

Fig. 2-27

Spacing for the Grandmother's Fan Dust Ruffle, showing the number of fans and approximate placement for each size.

Twin: two at the foot, two corner fans, four on each side; 13" between fans at the foot, 15" between fans at the sides

Full: three at the foot, two corner fans, four on each side; 13½" between fans at the foot, 15" between fans at sides

Queen: three at the foot, two corner fans, five on each side; 15" between fans at the foot, 12" between fans at sides

King: four at the foot, two corner fans, five on each side; 15½" between fans at the foot, 12" between fans at the sides

12. Serge or sew the pinned edges together with a ⅜" seam allowance. If sewing with a straight stitch, finish the seam allowance with a zigzag stitch or Fray-Check to prevent fraying. Machine topstitch along the sides of the quilted fans, catching the seam allowance to the wrong side of the fan.

13. For twin and full sizes, hem the two side edges with a narrow double-fold to the wrong side of the fabric. For queen and king sizes, serge or zigzag the side edge of the quilted fan at either end, turn the edge narrowly to the back side, and topstitch close to the edge to finish.

14. Sew a wide basting stitch about ¼" from the upper raw edge of the fabric insert sections only, leaving tails of thread at each end of the seam to gather it. Pull the tails of thread to gather each section to about 14"–15" wide. Leave these tails loose for adjustment later.

Note: If you are attaching this dust ruffle to the backing of a quilt or quilt-in-progress, omit the next steps and refer to the section on Attaching a Dust Ruffle to a Finished Quilt, Quilt-in-Progress, or Duvet Cover.

15. Cut the fabric for your dust ruffle platform 1" wider and 2" longer than the top of your box spring. Cut a slight curve at the corners of the foot end only, beginning about 1" before the corner and ending 1" beyond

the corner. Hem the top edge ("head" end) of the dust ruffle platform by turning it to the wrong side with a double fold and straight stitching to hold.

16. Pin the tops of the corner fans, face sides and raw edges together, to the curved corners of the foot end of the platform, easing them carefully around the curve (see Fig. 2-27).

17. Adjust the gathers of the fabric insert panels of the dust ruffle drop so it can be pinned evenly to fit the sides and foot end of the platform. Not counting the corner fans, the remaining fans should fit the platform as follows:

Twin: two at the foot, and four on each side
Full: three at the foot, and four on each side
Queen: three at the foot, and five on each side
King: four at the foot, five on each side

Obviously, the adjustment of the fans will vary slightly from size to size, but if they are evenly spaced, between the foot and along the sides, the finished dust ruffle will look beautiful, no matter what size you make. The adjustment between fans at the foot end will not necessarily be the same as the adjustment on the sides, but the difference will not have an adverse effect on the total look.

18. Sew the drop to the platform with a ⅜" seam allowance.

To Make This Dust Ruffle Using Any 12" Quilt Blocks

Materials Required

Face fabric: 2 yards each of two fabrics or ½ yard each of five to six fabric, depending on the quilt pattern(s) used

Insert panels: 1⅜ yards for all sizes

Backing and polyester batting: twin, 2½ yards each; full, 3 yards each; queen and king, 3½ yards each

Platforms: large flat sheet or 90" sheeting slightly longer and wider than the top of your box spring

Thread

Note: If you plan to attach this dust ruffle to the backing of a finished quilt or quilt-in-progress, you will need to slightly gather the top raw edges of the two quilt blocks placed at the curves of the foot end before pinning them in place.

Preparation and Construction

1. Cut and make the same number of 12" quilt blocks as the number of fans in the Grandmother's Fan Dust Ruffle for the size desired. Press.

2. Add border strips to the finished quilt blocks as described for the Shoo Fly Blocks Platform Dust Ruffle.

3. Cut polyester batting and backing the same size as the finished quilt blocks.

4. Place the quilt block and backing, face sides together, and lay the polyester batting on top.

5. Pin along the bottom edge and sew through all layers at the bottom edge only. Clip the seam allowance close the seam.

6. Turn right sides out, press, and sew through all layers around the three raw edges with a ¼" seam allowance. Machine or hand quilt along all patchwork seam lines.

7. Cut sections of insert fabric as described in Step 8 of the Grandmother's Fan Dust Ruffle, *except* cut pieces 15½" long by 8" wide, turning one 8" edge on each section with a ½" double-folded hem.

8. Align the hemmed edges of the insert pieces even with the finished edges of the quilt blocks, face sides and raw side edges together. Continue as described in Step 10 of the Grandmother's Fan Dust Ruffle.

9. Temporarily skip Step 11 of the Grandmother's Fan Dust Ruffle and continue with Steps 12–14, gathering the fabric insert sections to about 3" wide.

10. Determine the corner fans as described in Step 11.

11. Continue with Steps 15–18 of the Grandmother's Fan Dust Ruffle, substituting your quilted blocks for the fans.

Pillow Sham

Materials Required

Face fabric: 1 fat quarter yard (18" × 22") for the background of the fan; ⅓ yard for the triangles around the center square and two 4" × 21" side strips; ¼ yard each of 5–6 assorted fabrics for the fan

Lining and polyester batting: 22" × 28" of each

Backing fabric: ⅝ yard (2 pieces, 16" × 22" each)

Three yards of finished 2½"–3" ruffle for around the pillow sham

1 yard 1"-wide flat or ruffled lace for trim

Thread

Preparation and Construction

1. Transfer Fig. 2-18 onto tracing or freezer paper. Use the patterns in the actual size shown.

2. For each sham, cut one piece of pattern B, and using assorted fabrics, cut 6 of A. Sew them together as shown on Fig. 2-25, using ⅜" seam allowances.

3. Refer to Step 3 of the Grandmother's Fan Quilt for sewing on the lace.

4. Cut a 15¾" square from the background fabric. Place the fan, with edges even, in one corner of the square, pinning the raw edges together.

5. Baste the raw edges together with a ¼" seam allowance. Topstitch "in the ditch" between the lace and the fabric on the curved edge.

6. Cut two 12" squares from the ⅓ yard of fabric, and cut them in half diagonally, to get four triangles.

7. Sew the long edges of each triangle to each side of the fan square with ⅜" seam allowances.

8. Cut two strips from the remainder of the ⅓ yard of fabric, or from one of the other fabrics, 4" × 22". Sew these to the side edges of the square you just made, face sides and raw edges together, trimming any excess from the strips. Press.

9. Sandwich the polyester batting between the face and lining of the sham, with the fabrics face sides out.

10. Pin or baste the layers together and hand or machine quilt, following the seam lines on the face.

11. Baste around the raw edges, through all layers, with a narrow seam allowance.

12. Sew fabric ruffling around the entire outer edge of the finished sham face, right sides and raw edges together. Sew the ends together or overlap them and sew the ends into the seam allowance. Trim any excess lining, polyester batting, or ruffling from the edges.

13. Cut two pieces of backing fabric, 16" × 22". Sew a narrow double-folded hem to the wrong side on a 22" edge of each piece. Overlap the hemmed edges of these pieces by about 2", face sides up.

14. Lay the face of your pillow sham, face side down, on the overlapped backing and pin around all edges.

15. Sew around all edges with a ⅜" seam allowance. Trim off excess backing, clip the corners, and turn right side out.

This sham fits any standard bed pillow.

All-in-One Dust Ruffles

This is an easy and beautiful bedspread treatment that looks like a separate comforter and dust ruffle. It eliminates the tugging and shifting of conventional dust ruffles that slide out of place, and makes bedmaking a snap. This style is best suited to beds without a footboard.

Attaching a Dust Ruffle to a Quilt

The instructions listed below are for beds of any size or height.

For this treatment, you must purchase or make a dust ruffle that would fit a bed larger than your own. Only shirred or gathered dust ruffles are recommended. If making a dust ruffle, make the next size larger than your bed size—adjusting it for an exact fit will be explained later in the project. You will need only the dust ruffle drop, without the platform.

1. Start by folding your finished quilt, or quilt or duvet cover backing, in half lengthwise to find a center line that extends from the head of the bed to the foot. Press this fold, or draw a line down the center mark with an erasable marking pen or chalk, on the face side of the backing.

2. Next, measure the width of the top of your bed, and the height from the floor to the top of your mattress (Fig. 2-28). Be sure to remove all covers from your bed before taking measurements. If you have not yet made or purchased a dust ruffle, I suggest using one that has no less than a 16" drop for beds 22" or taller. You may add a 2¾"-wide strip of fabric to the top edge of a finished dust ruffle for added length, if needed.

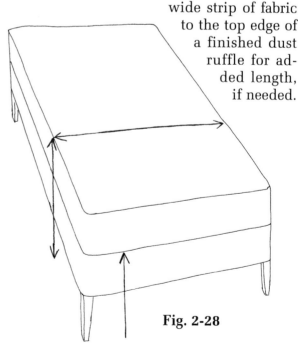

Fig. 2-28

This strip will be hidden underneath the quilt when sewn in place. The dust ruffles shown in this book finish at 14" long, with a ³⁄₈" seam allowance at the top edge. A 2¾" strip added to this with a ³⁄₈" seam allowance would give the necessary two extra inches for tall beds, with a ³⁄₈" seam allowance remaining for attaching it.

3. The following formula will determine where your dust ruffle will be placed on the backing:

> (Bed width + height + height − dust ruffle drop length − dust ruffle drop length) ÷ 2
> = measurement from the center line to the side edge
> or
> [Width + 2 (height) − 2 (dust ruffle drop)] ÷ 2 = final measurement

For example:

If your bed is 54" wide and stands 24" tall and the dust ruffle you wish to attach is 16" (not counting a ³⁄₈" or so seam allowance on the dust ruffle), your formula would look like this:

> (54" + 24" + 24" - 16" - 16") ÷ 2 = 35

4. The number you end up with is the measurement you will take from the center line of the backing towards each side of the quilt. Mark a line for this measurement the length of the backing, from the top edge, to a few inches from the foot (Fig. 2-29). If your

backing is not at least 3" wider on each side than this measurement, add a strip to your dust ruffle, as described earlier, to lengthen it, then re-calculate your measurements.

5. Measure the space between the lines you have just drawn and the edges of your quilt. This amount should be equal on both sides. Measure the same number from the foot edge of your bed and draw a line across the foot end. This will allow for equal and balanced drop lengths of your quilt and dust ruffle around the entire edge of your bed (see Fig. 2-29).

6. Place a large plate on the inside corners of the drawn lines that meet at the foot end of the backing. Draw a curved line for the dust ruffle placement (Fig. 2-30). You are now ready to attach your dust ruffle.

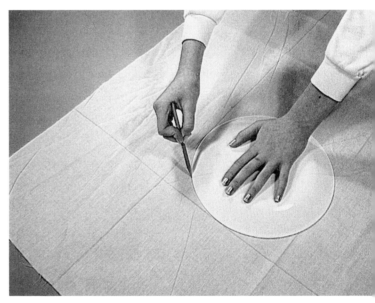

Fig. 2-30

7. Measure the total overall length of the lines that mark the dust ruffle placement on the backing. Measure the upper raw edge of the dust ruffle to be used. Adjust the dust ruffle to fit the lines by adding or loosening gathers, or cut some off if there is quite a bit of excess. Add 1-2" on the dust ruffle at each side of the "head" end, to allow for hems. If your dust ruffle will be detachable, place bias tape over the raw upper edge of the dust ruffle for a clean finish.

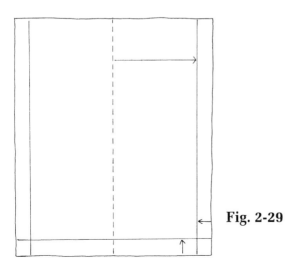

Fig. 2-29

Permanent Attachment to a Quilt-in-Progress or Duvet Cover

1. Serge or zigzag the upper raw edge of the dust ruffle to keep it from fraying.

2. Pin the upper edge of the finished dust ruffle on the line you have drawn on the backing, with the backing face side up, and the dust ruffle face side down.

3. Extend the dust ruffle an inch or two from the top edge and leave a bit of the end of it loose to allow it to be hemmed later. Do this at the beginning and end of the dust ruffle. (Fig. 2-31 shows one side extended and one side already hemmed.)

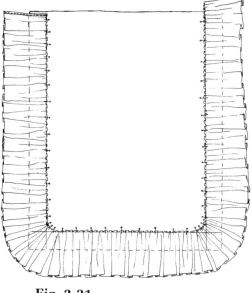

Fig. 2-31

4. You may adjust your dust ruffle to fit exactly by taking a few extra tucks and gathers as you pin it in place, or loosen excess tucks or gathers to lengthen it.

Note: The bottom edge of the dust ruffle should extend beyond the outside edge of the backing, not toward the inside.

5. Sew the dust ruffle to the backing using a straight stitch, and following the upper edge of the dust ruffle.

This treatment can be used on the duvet cover backing described earlier in the chapter. Because the dust ruffle is attached so close to the outer edges of the backing, there

is still plenty of space in which to insert your comforter. Simply sew over the overlapped edges as though they were not there.

After the dust ruffle has been sewn in place, finish the two ends at the top edge with a narrow, double-folded hem.

Detachable Dust Ruffle

1. To make your dust ruffle detachable, measure and pin it in place as described in Method #1. Instead of sewing it permanently, place marks about 6" apart along the upper bias-taped edge of the dust ruffle and on the line on the backing.

2. Glue (using fabric glue or a glue gun), or machine stitch to an unfinished quilt backing, or hand stitch through only the backing of a finished quilt half of a set of hook-and-loop tabs or a ½" button on each of the marks made on the line on the backing (Fig. 2-32).

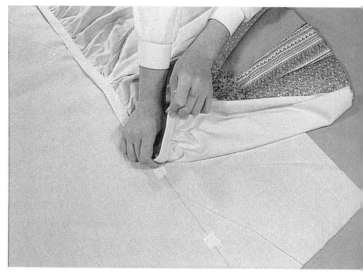

Fig. 2-32

3. On the face side of the bias-taped edge of the dust ruffle, sew the other half of the hook-and-loop tabs at each mark, or machine stitch buttonholes to fit the buttons.

4. Hem the two remaining raw edges that will be at the top edge of the quilt with a narrow, double-folded hem.

3

The Kitchen and Dining Room

Quilts in the dining room? Yes! What better way is there to satisfy your hunger for peaceful beauty and charm than to use quilted accessories in the room in which you are nourished?

By their very nature, quilts portray a sense of tradition and family values. Make a beautiful memory for your family with quilted accessories for your kitchen and dining room.

Trip Around the World

These wonderful table accessories can create an assortment of fun and unusual dining experiences. Each place setting can represent a different country, with the Trip Around the World tablecloth representing the earth. Everyone is earth conscious and hungering for a peaceful, united world. Why not show it at your dinner table?

Perhaps a meal will feature the cuisine of a particular country, and matching place mats from the country would be appropriate. Or let your children decide where in the world they want to eat, and use it as a learning tool. Just think of all the exciting things you can do with these wonderful accessories!

Patchwork Tablecloth

This patchwork cloth in color Fig. 11 finishes to 60" × 60" or 60" × 88", and you can trim it or add to it to fit the size you need. It's so easy to make, you will want one in colors for every season and every holiday. Materials and dimensions in parentheses are for the larger tablecloth (60" × 88").

Materials Required

Face fabric, 44/45" wide: 1 yard each of four fabric (1½ yards each) strongly contrasting colors, with a mix of large prints, small prints, and solids or mini-prints

Backing: large flat sheet, wide sheeting fabric, or fabric that has been seamed to fit 62" × 62" (62" × 90")

Thread

Preparation and Construction

1. From the width of your face fabric, cut strips 4¼" wide, using a rotary cutter and clear plastic ruler. You will need eight (twelve) strips of each color. Stack the strips neatly in sets of four, trim the selvage close to one end, and make one 4¼"-wide cut from each set of strips, to make eight (twelve) 4¼" squares of each color. (Only ten will be used for the larger size.)

2. Using ⅜" seam allowances throughout your project, sew the remaining length of the strips together as shown in Fig. 3-1. Make two (three) of each of these sets. Press the seam allowances toward the darker fabric.

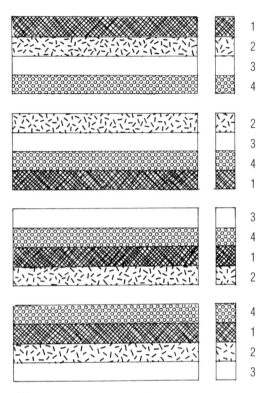

Fig. 3-1

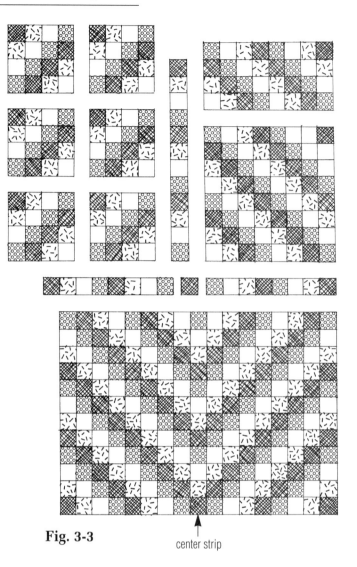

Fig. 3-3

center strip

3. Carefully layer these sets and trim one end evenly, cutting through the seams. Continue to cut through the seams, the entire length of the strips, using 4¼" spacing between cuts.

4. Arrange these sets of fabrics as shown in Fig. 3-2 and sew them together into sixteen (twenty-four) blocks, using ⅜" seam allowances.

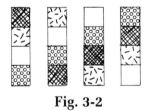

Fig. 3-2

5. Sew the loose 4¼" squares (from Step 1) into strips as shown in Fig. 3-3. Remove one square of fabric 1 from an extra set of cut strips that remains after piecing your blocks. Use this as the center square of the long strip or cut one extra 4¼" square of fabric 1.

6. Arrange the blocks as shown in Fig. 3-3. Sew these together to complete each of the four "corners" as shown in Fig. 3-4. Connect the corners with the shorter center strips,

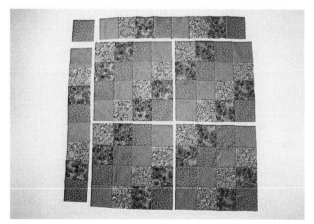

Fig. 3-4

making two halves. Join the two halves with the remaining long center strip between them. Press all seams.

7. On a large flat surface, lay your backing fabric face side up. Lay the pieced top of your tablecloth face side down. Trim the backing equal to the face and pin around all sides.

8. Sew around all sides with ⅜" seam allowance, leaving an opening about 18" wide on one side. Clip the corners and turn face side out.

9. Turn the edges of the opening to the inside, ⅜", and hand stitch or topstitch to close. Press around the edges.

10. If you wish, topstitch, as though you were quilting, along all seam lines. This helps to prevent fraying of the inside seam allowances when the tablecloth is washed.

Flags of the World Place Mats

These easy-to-make 13" × 19" place mats will keep the conversation lively at your dinner table (see color Fig. 10). Although they represent a very small corner of the world, you can use these as a starting point for your own United Nations table. There may be minor variances in the flags shown from the true flag for a particular country because the size of the place mat may not be completely proportional.

Materials Required

You will need a fat quarter yard (18" × 22") of each of the solid colors shown for each flag (@ = appliqué pieces; * = 13¾" × 19¾" piece) or ½ yard each if fat quarters are unavailable (except regular ¼ yards of red and white for Great Britain).

Australia: Red, white, royal blue *@
Canada: Red, white @
Great Britain: Red, white, royal blue *@
France: Red, white, royal blue
Greece: Sky blue, white

Iceland: Red, white, royal blue *@
Ireland: Orange, white, green
Italy: Red, white, green
New Zealand: Red, white, royal blue *@
Norway: Red*, white, royal blue @
United States: Red, white, royal blue @
13¾" × 19¾" rectangle of backing and polyester batting (optional) for each place mat
Paper-backed fusible web for patterns with appliqué pieces (indicated by @)
Thread
Freezer or tracing paper for making your pattern

Preparation and Construction

There are seven patterns for the eleven flags shown above. France, Italy, and Ireland share the same pattern, as do Australia/New Zealand and Norway/Iceland.

1. Cut your backing and polyester batting (optional) to 13¾" × 19¾".

2. Cut face fabric 13¾" × 19¾" from the * fabric for the following flags: Australia, England, Iceland, New Zealand, and Norway.

3. Full-size patterns are provided for appliqué and patchwork pieces. Press paper-backed fusible web to the wrong side of fabrics that will be used for appliqué.

All appliqué patterns are shown the exact finished size, without added seam allowances, for satin stitching them by machine with a narrow, closely set zigzag stitch. If you plan to hand appliqué your pieces, omit the paper-backed fusible web and add ¼" seam allowances to all sides. All patchwork patterns have a ⅜" seam allowance included.

4. Transfer necessary pattern pieces onto tracing or freezer paper. Cut the required pieces as described with the pattern. Many pieces are strip cut, without patterns. Following are instructions for the individual flags. Refer to "Finishing Your Place Mat" on page 45 to complete the project.

41

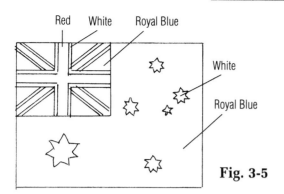

Red   White   Royal Blue

White

Royal Blue

Fig. 3-5

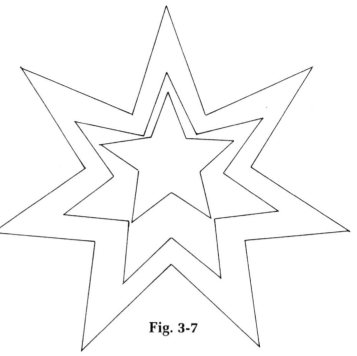

Fig. 3-7

Australia

1. Press paper-backed fusible web to the wrong side of the red and white fabrics. Cut two 1"-wide stripes of white, and two ½"-wide red stripes, each 12" long. Fold the blue rectangle in half, finger press the crease, then fold it in half the opposite way, finger pressing the crease to define four equal quarters of the flag. Place the stripes in an X, with the red centered on top of the white, in the upper left quarter.

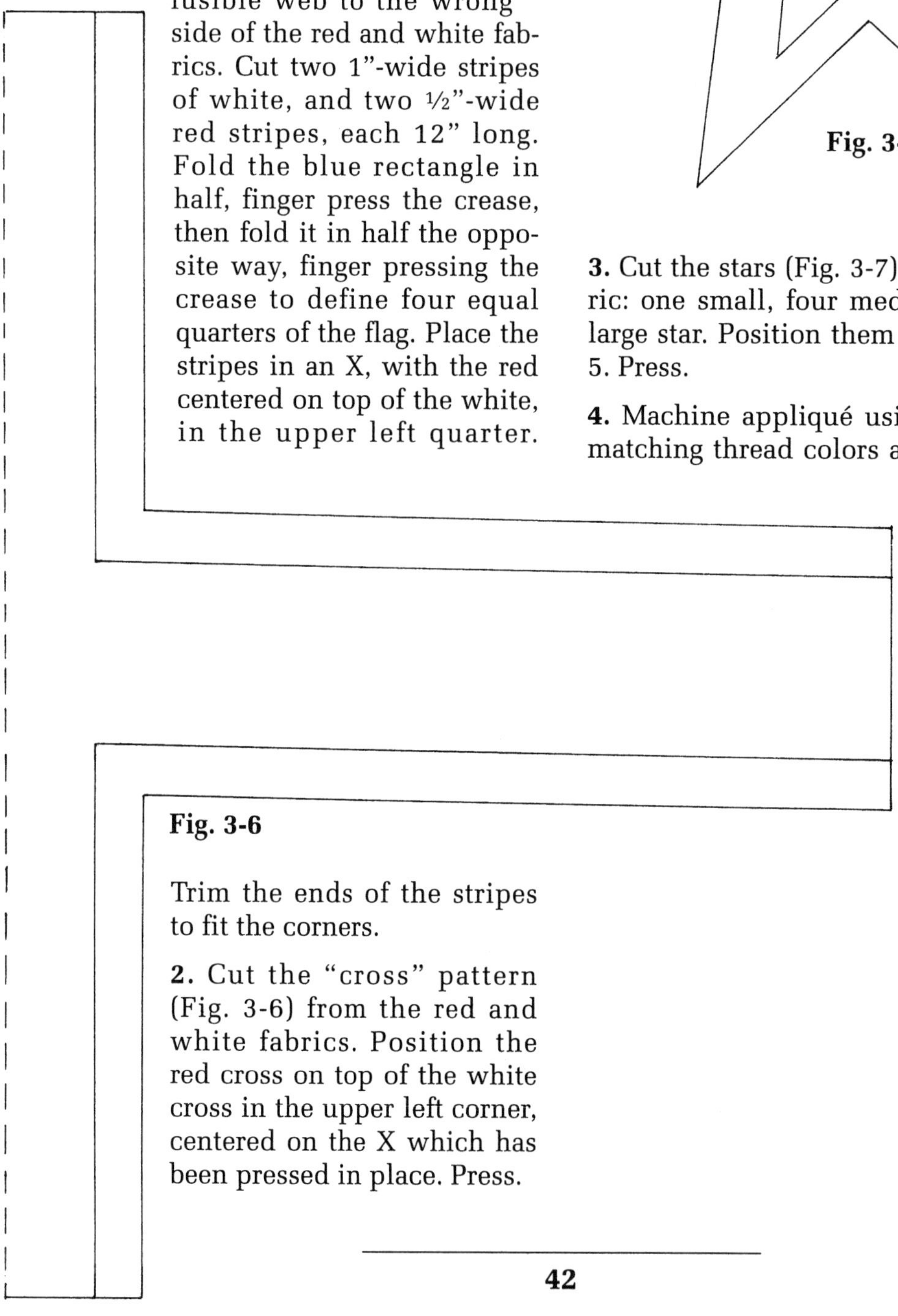

Fig. 3-6

Trim the ends of the stripes to fit the corners.

2. Cut the "cross" pattern (Fig. 3-6) from the red and white fabrics. Position the red cross on top of the white cross in the upper left corner, centered on the X which has been pressed in place. Press.

3. Cut the stars (Fig. 3-7) from the white fabric: one small, four medium stars, and one large star. Position them as shown in Fig. 3-5. Press.

4. Machine appliqué using a satin stitch in matching thread colors along all visible raw edges of the pieces that have been pressed in place.

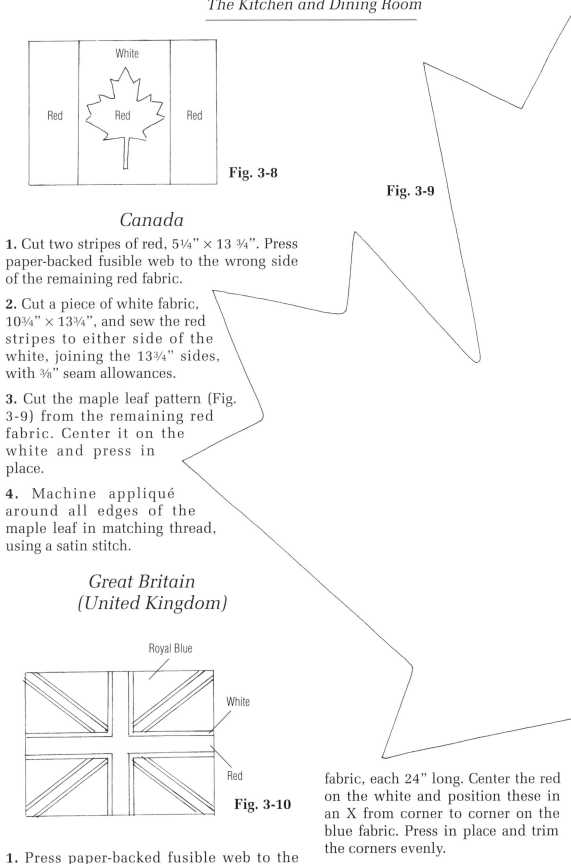

Fig. 3-8

Fig. 3-9

Canada

1. Cut two stripes of red, 5¼" × 13 ¾". Press paper-backed fusible web to the wrong side of the remaining red fabric.

2. Cut a piece of white fabric, 10¾" × 13¾", and sew the red stripes to either side of the white, joining the 13¾" sides, with ⅜" seam allowances.

3. Cut the maple leaf pattern (Fig. 3-9) from the remaining red fabric. Center it on the white and press in place.

4. Machine appliqué around all edges of the maple leaf in matching thread, using a satin stitch.

Great Britain (United Kingdom)

Fig. 3-10

1. Press paper-backed fusible web to the wrong side of the red and the white fabric.

2. Cut two 1¾"-wide stripes from the white fabric, and two 1"-wide stripes from the red

fabric, each 24" long. Center the red on the white and position these in an X from corner to corner on the blue fabric. Press in place and trim the corners evenly.

3. Cut two 1½"-wide strips of red, one at 13¾" long and one 19¾" long. Cut two 2½"-wide stripes of white the same lengths as the red.

4. With the red centered on the white, position these in a cross on top of the X, as shown in Fig. 3-10.

5. Machine appliqué in matching thread colors along all raw edges, using a satin stitch.

France

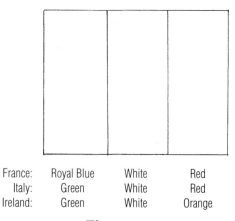

France:	Royal Blue	White	Red
Italy:	Green	White	Red
Ireland:	Green	White	Orange

Fig. 3-11

Cut one piece of each color, 7¼" × 13¾". Position them as shown in Fig. 3-11, and sew them together along the 13¾" sides with ⅜" seam allowances.

Greece

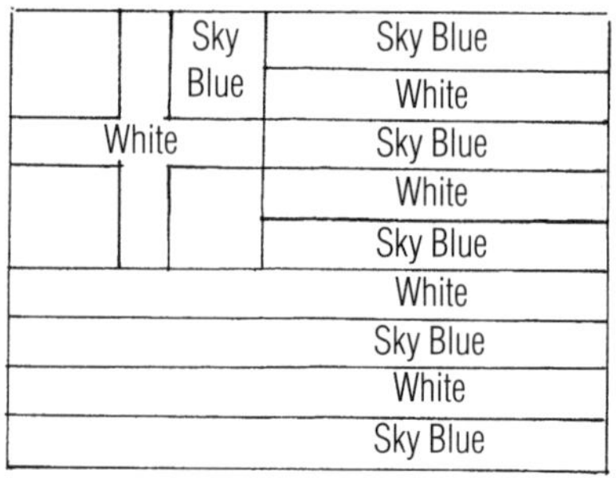

Fig. 3-12

1. Cut two stripes each of white and sky blue, 2¼" × 19¾", and sew them together, alternating colors, using ⅜" seam allowances.

2. Cut three stripes of blue, 2¼" × 12¼", and two stripes of white, 2¼" × 12¼. Sew these together with ⅜" seam allowances

alternating colors, and starting and ending with blue.

3. Cut four blue 3¾" squares. Cut two pieces of white, 2¼" × 3¾", and sew each white piece between two squares of blue, making two sets of stripes.

4. Cut one stripe of white, 2¼" × 8¼", and sew this between the two sets of stripes, to create a white cross on a ground of blue.

5. Sew the cross square to the end of the set of 12¼" long stripes. Position the remaining 19¾" long stripes so the white stripe is sewn to the lower edge of the first set, with the cross in the upper left corner.

Iceland

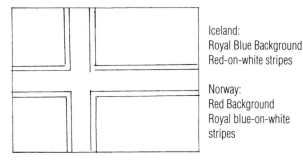

| Iceland: |
| Royal Blue Background |
| Red-on-white stripes |
| |
| Norway: |
| Red Background |
| Royal blue-on-white stripes |

Fig. 3-13

1. Press paper-backed fusible web to the wrong side of the red fabric only.

2. From the blue cut two 5½" squares and two rectangles, 5½" × 11½".

3. Cut two white pieces, 4¼" × 5½". Sew a blue square to one 5½" side of each white piece, and a 5½" side of each rectangle to the opposite side of each white piece, using ⅜" seam allowances.

4. Cut a white stripe, 4¼" × 19¾". Sew this stripe between the two sets of blue/white, positioning the squares and rectangles opposite each other.

5. Cut a stripe of the red fabric, 2" × 13¾", and one 2" × 19¾". Center these red stripes on the white stripes of the same length.

6. Machine appliqué the edges of the red stripes using a satin stitch.

Ireland

Follow the directions for the French flag, substituting green for blue and orange for red.

Italy

Follow the directions for the French flag, substituting green for blue.

New Zealand

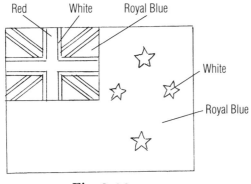

Fig. 3-14

Follow the direction for the Australian flag, except use the pattern for the stars for the flag of New Zealand (Fig. 3-15), and position them as shown in Fig. 3-14.

Fig. 3-15

Norway

Follow the directions for the flag of Iceland, reversing the blue and red fabrics.

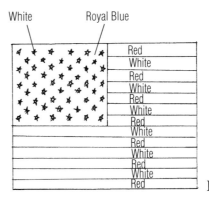

Fig. 3-16

United States

1. Cut three stripes each of red and white, 1¾" × 19 ¾. Sew these together on the long edges, using ⅜" seam allowances, alternating the colors.

2. Cut four red stripes and three white stripes, each 1¾" × 11¾". Sew these together on the long edges with ⅜" seam allowances, starting and ending with a red stripe.

3. Cut a rectangle of blue fabric, 9¼" × 7¾". Sew a 7¾" edge of this rectangle to a 7¾" edge of the 11¾"-long stripes.

4. Sew the white end stripe of the 19¾" set of stripes to this rectangle/stripe set, positioning the rectangle in the upper left corner.

5. Press paper-backed fusible web to the remaining white fabric, and cut 50 stars from this fabric using the pattern in Fig. 3-17.

Fig. 3-17

6. Position the stars on the blue fabric as shown in Fig. 3-16. Press them in place, and machine appliqué around the edges using a satin stitch.

Finishing Your Place Mats

1. Place the backing right sides together on the face of your place mat. Trim it, if necessary, so they are equal in size. If you plan to line your place mat with polyester batting, cut it to the same size and place it on top of these. Pin around all edges.

2. Sew around all edges using a ⅜" seam allowance, leaving an opening about 6" wide on one side. Trim the seams, clip the corners, and turn the place mat face sides out through the opening.

3. Turn the edges of the opening to the inside and hand stitch or topstitch to close.

4. Hand or machine quilt along seam lines to finish.

Morning Glory Kitchen/Breakfast Nook

Bring a bit of sunshine and beautiful blooms into your kitchen with this versatile appliqué motif (color Figs. 8 and 9). A simple basic flower pattern can be reversed and repositioned to create a variety of designs.

Patterns and directions shown are for machine appliquéing using a satin stitch (a narrow, closely set zigzag). Machine appliqué will give durability and washability to these projects. Hand appliquéing is not recommended as it is best suited to projects that aren't handled or washed regularly.

Materials Required

Assorted fabrics to be used for the appliqué pieces

Background fabric: 1 yard each for appliance covers and chair pads, and ½ yard each for hot pads/oven mitts, place mats, etc.

Backing and polyester batting in the same amounts as the background fabric

Thread in colors to match the appliqué pieces, as well as to match the background fabric

Paper-backed fusible web

Double-fold bias tape or ruffling as needed for each project (about 2 yards each)

Preparation and Construction

1. Transfer the pattern (Fig. 3-18) to tracing paper or template plastic, and cut them out.

2. Press paper-backed fusible web to the wrong side of fabrics to be used for the flowers and leaves.

3. Place these fabrics face-to-face or back-to-back and cut assorted reverse images of each pattern piece to give variety in the placement of the flowers and leaves.

Appliance Covers

These small appliance covers are constructed using the same basic steps, but with different sized pieces. The front and back of the cover is cut the same size for each appliance, with an insert section of fabric separating the two. Cut face fabric, backing fabric, and polyester batting in the following dimensions for each appliance:

Two-slice toaster: front and back, 12" × 8"; insert, 6" × 29"

Blender: front and back, 8" × 16"; insert: 8" × 41"

Electric can opener: front and back, 8" × 9"; insert: 6" × 27"

Coffeemaker/Mixer: front and back: 12" × 15"; insert 12" × 43"

Do **Steps 1–3** of the Morning Glory Kitchen/Breakfast Nook.

4. Arrange your appliqué cutouts on the face fabric for the front of your appliance cover. When positioning your appliqué, note that in the dimensions given in the preceding list, the second measurement represents the height of the appliance cover. Pin, press, or glue in place. Add leaves and buds. Use a chalk pencil or erasable fabric marker to fill in stems and curlicues as shown in the color photographs.

5. Machine appliqué around all edges and on all lines, using a narrow, closely set zigzag stitch, in a color similar to the fabric you are stitching around, and in a color that matches the leaves for the stems and curlicues.

Fig. 3-18

6. Layer this piece with backing fabric and polyester batting of the same size, with the fabrics face sides out and the polyester batting sandwiched between them, and machine quilt around the appliqué.

7. Layer the face fabric, backing, and polyester batting for the back and the insert section and machine quilt these layers with straight lines or grids.

8. Pin a long edge of the insert section, backing sides and raw edges together, to the top and two sides (height) of the front of your appliance cover. Serge or sew these edges together with a ⅜" seam allowance (see Fig. 3-19). The seam will be on the face side.

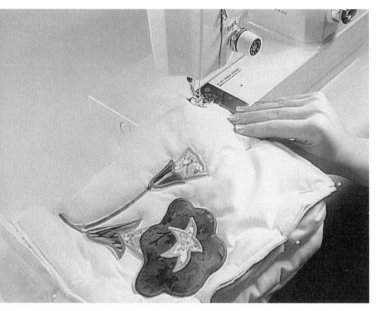

Fig. 3-19

9. Repeat this for the back of the appliance cover.

10. Sew bias tape around the seams to cover them.

11. Place your cover over your appliance before finishing the bottom edge. Trim any excess height as desired by cutting from the bottom raw edge. Serge or straight stitch close to the edge.

12. Sew double-fold bias tape around the entire bottom edge, leaving about 2" extra at the end. Fold under about 1" of the extra, and stitch down.

Chair Pad and Seat Back

This lovely set is designed to fit almost any kitchen/dining chair. The unique seat back is made with two-way stretch spandex on the back for a snug, stay-put fit on any chair.

You will need ¼ yard of two-way stretch spandex-type material for the seat back. You will also need one yard of extra fabric of your choice for the ruffles on both, plus extra polyester batting for cushioning, and fabric for lining.

Preparation and Construction

Do **Steps 1-3** of the Morning Glory Kitchen/Breakfast Nook.

4. Cut a 17" square of each of the face and backing fabrics for the chair pad. Cut a 9" × 15" rectangle of each for the seat back.

5. Arrange your appliqué pieces on the face fabrics, and pin, press, or glue them in place. Add leaves, buds, and curlicues using a chalk pencil or erasable marking pen as described in Steps 4 and 5 of the Morning Glory Appliance Covers.

6. Machine appliqué around all edges and on all lines, using a narrow, closely set zigzag stitch.

7. To make the ruffles: Cut five 6"-wide strips from the width of your extra fabric. Sew them together on the short ends to make a long strip of 6"-wide fabric. Fold the strip in half lengthwise, wrong sides together, so the raw edges meet the right sides face out. Press the fold. With a basting stitch, sew about ¼" from the raw edge. Pull the basting thread to gather the ruffle to about half of its original length.

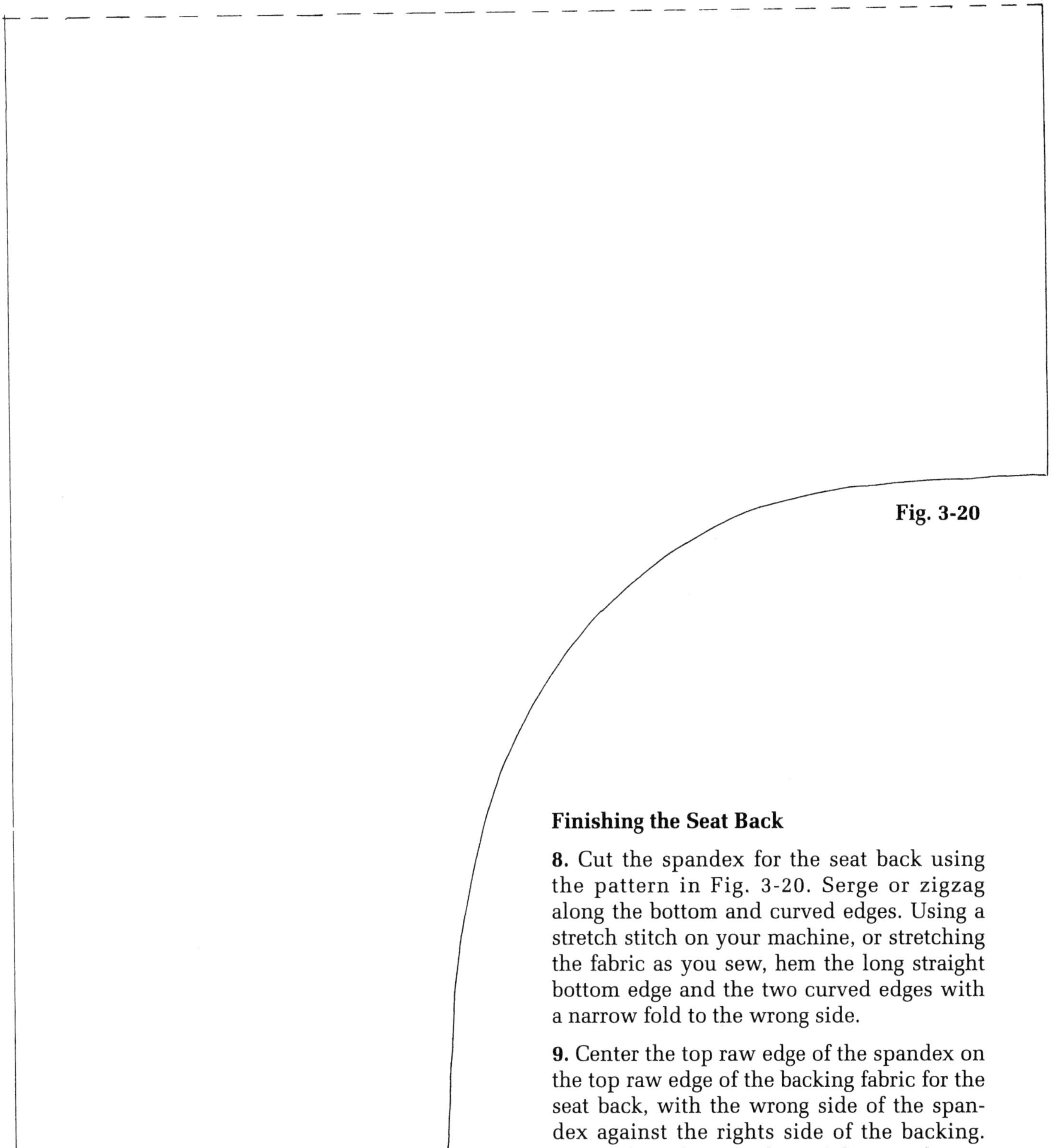

Fig. 3-20

Finishing the Seat Back

8. Cut the spandex for the seat back using the pattern in Fig. 3-20. Serge or zigzag along the bottom and curved edges. Using a stretch stitch on your machine, or stretching the fabric as you sew, hem the long straight bottom edge and the two curved edges with a narrow fold to the wrong side.

9. Center the top raw edge of the spandex on the top raw edge of the backing fabric for the seat back, with the wrong side of the spandex against the rights side of the backing. Center the side raw edges of the spandex on the side raw edges of the backing. Baste these together along the edges with a ¼" seam allowance. Note that the spandex is slightly larger than the backing and will gap a bit. The bottom edge of the spandex will

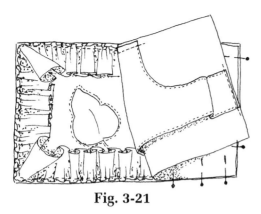

Fig. 3-21

be above the bottom edge of the backing, as shown in Fig. 3-21.

10. Cut two pieces of polyester batting the same size as the face/backing fabrics of your seat back. Sandwich one of these pieces between the face and a lining fabric cut to the same size, right sides out. Pin the edges to hold them in place, and machine quilt around the appliqué.

11. With raw edges together, sew the ruffle around the entire appliquéd and quilted face of the seat back. Open the basting seam slightly, and sew right sides of the ruffle together where the ends meet.

12. Place the spandex/backing, right sides together, on the face of the seat back, tucking the ruffle in all around.

13. Place the remaining rectangle of polyester batting on top of the backing, and re-pin around the edges through all layers.

14. Sew around all edges with a ½" seam allowance, leaving an opening at the bottom about 7" wide. Trim the seam allowance, clip the corners, and turn right side out.

15. Cut 8" × 14" rectangles of polyester batting and slide them neatly inside the seat back until it is as thick as you like. You may substitute a 7" × 13" rectangle of ½"-thick foam if you prefer.

16. Turn the raw edges of the opening to the inside and hand stitch or machine topstitch to close. If you want to be able to remove the inside layers when washing the chair pads, sew hook-and-loop tape (Velcro) to the seam allowances of the opening.

Finishing the Chair Pad

17. Cut two pieces of polyester batting the same size as the face of your chair pad. Sandwich one of these pieces between the appliquéd face and a lining fabric cut to the same size, right sides out. Machine quilt around the appliqué.

18. With raw edges together, sew the ruffle around the entire appliquéd and quilted face of the chair pad. Open the basting seam slightly, and sew right sides of the ruffle together where the ends meet.

19. Cut two strips of background fabric, 44" × 5". Hem around all sides of both strips with a narrow double fold, or a rolled hem if you have the proper attachment for your machine. Fold each strip in half, matching the short ends, and make a pleat at the fold.

20. Place this pleated fold at the top (or what will be the back edge) of your chair pad, with the pleated fold at the raw edge and the tie ends toward the center of the square (Fig. 3-22). Place these near the corners, about ½" from the side edges, right sides together. Pin to hold.

Fig. 3-22

21. Place the face and backing, right sides together, carefully tucking in the ruffle and tie ends.

22. Place the remaining square of polyester batting against the wrong side of the backing. Pin around the edges through all layers.

23. Starting on one of the folded tie ends, sew around the entire piece with a ½" seam allowance, ending on the other tie end. Leave an opening between the ties at the back edge. Trim the seam allowances, clip the corners, and turn right sides out.

24. Cut 15"–16" squares of polyester batting and slide them neatly inside the chair pad until it is as thick as you like. You may substitute a 15" square of 1"-thick foam for sturdier cushioning.

25. Turn the raw edges of the opening to the inside and hand stitch, or machine topstitch to close. If you want to be able to remove the inside layers when washing the chair pads, sew hook-and-loop tape (Velcro) to the seam allowances of the opening.

Place Mat

For each place mat, you will need an extra ¼ yard of a fabric of your choice for ruffles.

Preparation and Construction

Do **Steps 1–3** of the Morning Glory Kitchen/Breakfast Nook.

4. For each place mat, cut two rectangles of background fabric, 13" × 19". Arrange appliqué pieces on the face side of one of these rectangles and pin, press, or glue in place. Add leaves, buds, and curlicues, using a chalk pencil or erasable marking pen as described in Steps 4 and 5 of the Morning Glory appliance covers.

5. Machine appliqué around all edges and on all lines, using a narrow, closely set zigzag stitch.

6. Cut three 3"-wide strips from the width of the extra fabric of your choice. Sew these together at the short ends, right sides together, to make a long circle of fabric. Fold this in half lengthwise, with face sides out and raw edges together. Press.

7. Sew a basting stitch along the raw edge with a ¼" seam allowance. Pull the basting thread to gather the fabric evenly, equal to the size of the outer edge of the place mat. Pin the ruffle to the appliquéd face, right sides and raw edges together. Sew the ruffle in place with a ⅜" seam allowance.

8. Place the remaining rectangle of fabric, right sides together, on the ruffled face. Cut a rectangle of polyester batting equal in size, and place it on top of these. Pin around all edges to hold.

9. Sew around all edges with a ⅜" seam allowance, leaving an opening about 6" wide on one side. Trim the seams, clip the corners, and turn the place mat face sides out through the opening.

10. Turn the edges of the opening to the inside and hand stitch or topstitch to close.

11. Machine quilt around the appliqué to finish.

Table Runner

Standard lengths for table runners are 36", 54" and 72". You will need 1 yard, 1½ yards, or 2 yards, respectively, of face fabric for each of these sizes, and ⅓ yard, ½ yard, and ¾ yard, respectively, of extra fabric of your choice for the ruffles.

Preparation and Construction

Do **Steps 1–3** of the Morning Glory Kitchen/Breakfast Nook.

4. Cut two rectangles 13" wide by the desired length. Arrange appliqué pieces on the face side of one of these rectangles and pin, press, or glue in place. Add leaves, buds, and curlicues, using a chalk pencil or erasable marking pen as described in Steps 4 and 5 of the Morning Glory appliance covers.

5. Cut four 3"-wide strips from the width of the extra fabric of your choice for the 36"-long table runner, six strips for the 54"-long table runner, and eight strips for the 72"-long table runner. Continue with the instructions after the first sentence in Step 6 of the Morning Glory place mat and complete your table runner as described in Steps 7 through 11, except leave an opening about 10" (instead of 6") wide in Step 9 to accommodate the extra bulk.

Hot Pad and Oven Mitt

You may wish to substitute heat-resistant, Teflon-coated fabric for the backing. Nancy's Notions sewing supply catalog offers Teflon-coated fabric called Iron Quick for heat-resistant pads and oven mitts.

Hot Pad

Preparation and Construction

Do **Steps 1–3** of the Morning Glory Kitchen/Breakfast Nook.

4. Cut one square of face fabric and one square of backing or Teflon-coated fabric, 8" × 8" each.

5. Arrange fabric appliqué pieces on the face fabric. Add leaves, buds, and curlicues, using a chalk pencil or erasable marking pen as described in Steps 4 and 5 of the Morning Glory appliance covers. Pin, press, or glue in place.

6. Machine appliqué around all edges and on all lines, using a narrow, closely set zigzag stitch.

7. Cut two layers of polyester batting the same size as the squares. Layer the polyester batting between the backing and face fabrics with the fabrics right sides out.

8. Machine quilt around appliqué pieces.

9. Serge or zigzag stitch around the raw edges. Cover the edges with bias tape, finishing the last end by folding it to the wrong side and overlapping the first edge.

10. Add a loop at one corner for hanging the hot pad, if desired. Straight stitch 3" of double-fold bias tape along the folds to make a tail, fold it in half, turning the raw ends to the inside. Position this at one corner of your hot pad and machine tack in place.

Oven Mitt

Preparation and Construction

Do **Steps 1–3** of the Morning Glory Kitchen/Breakfast Nook.

4. Transfer the mitt pattern (Fig. 3-23) to tracing paper and cut one each of the face fabric and backing or Teflon-coated fabric. Cut two each of lining fabric and four each of polyester batting.

5. Arrange the appliqué pieces on the face fabric, taking care to note whether your mitt will be left-handed or right-handed. Add leaves, buds, and curlicues, using a chalk pencil or erasable marking pen as described in Steps 4 and 5 of the Morning Glory appliance covers. Pin, press, or glue in place.

6. Machine appliqué around all edges and on all lines, using a narrow, closely set zigzag stitch.

7. Layer the appliquéd face and one lining piece, face sides out, with two layers of polyester batting between. Do the same with the remaining pieces, reversing the backing and lining fabrics so the backing fabric and face fabric are right sides out when layered together after quilting.

8. Machine quilt around the appliqué pieces on the face side, and in straight lines or a grid pattern on the backing.

9. Place these quilted pieces, lining sides together, and serge or zigzag around the edges, leaving the bottom straight edges open.

10. Add double-fold bias tape around the serged edges, then finish the bottom edges with bias tape as well, as described in Step 12 of the Morning Glory appliance covers. Add a fabric loop as described in Step 10 of the hot pad instructions, if desired.

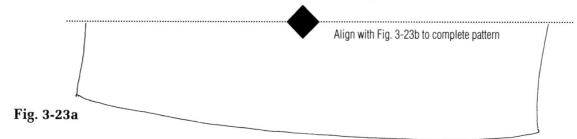

Align with Fig. 3-23b to complete pattern

Fig. 3-23a

Fig. 3-23b

Quilt Square Apron, Potholders, and Place Mats

Of course, your quilted kitchen accessories wouldn't be complete without a lovely apron, potholders, and place mat. And these little 4" quilt blocks can be interchanged and re-arranged in so many ways. What a great gift idea!

Materials Needed

Apron: 1¼ yards of "base" fabric (for the skirt and ties); ¼ yard each of 4–5 fabrics for the quilt squares; ¼ yard backing fabric (behind the quilt blocks); ¼ yard polyester batting; thread

Potholders: ¼ yard each of 4–5 fabrics for quilt squares; ¼ yard of backing or heat-resistant, Teflon-coated fabric; ¼ yard polyester batting; thread

Place mats, set of 4: ¼ yard each of 4–5 fabrics for the quilt squares; ¾ yard backing and polyester batting; thread

Preparation and Construction

1. Transfer the quilt block patterns (Figs. 3-24 to 3-27) to tracing or other paper. Cut the necessary number of pieces for each quilt block, as shown with the directions for that block. Patterns show the number of pieces needed for a single block. You will need four quilt blocks for each potholder, twelve quilt blocks for the bib and two pockets on the apron, and twenty quilt blocks for each place mat. Mix and match them as you wish.

2. Sew your blocks together according to the diagrams and directions shown with each block, using ¼" seam allowances.

3. Sew the finished small blocks together in sets of four, to complete 8½" squares for the potholders and apron. For place mat requirements, refer to the instructions for To Finish a Place Mat on page 57.

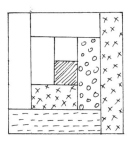

Fig. 3-24

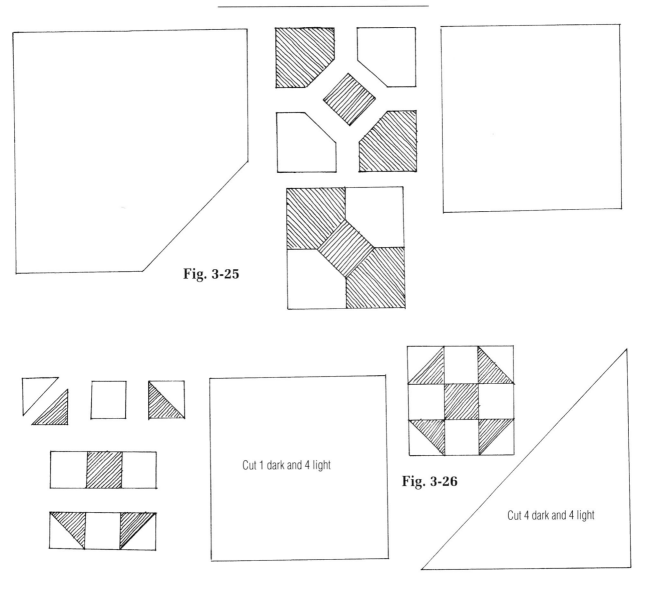

Fig. 3-25

Fig. 3-26

Cut 1 dark and 4 light

Cut 4 dark and 4 light

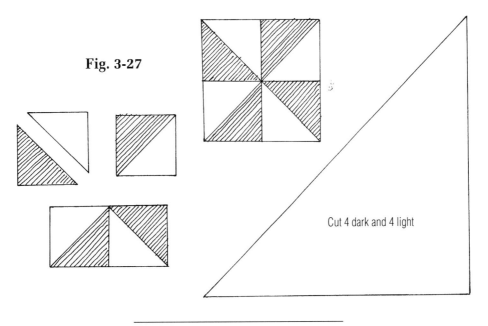

Fig. 3-27

Cut 4 dark and 4 light

To Finish a Potholder

4. Cut backing or heat-resistant, Teflon-coated fabric, and two squares of polyester batting, equal to the size of your finished quilt square.

5. Place the fabrics face sides together with polyester batting on either side. Pin around the edges through all layers.

6. Sew around three sides with a ¼" seam allowance. Trim the seams and clip the corners. Turn face sides out.

7. Turn the raw edges ¼" to the inside and pin to hold.

8. Cut a piece of fabric 3" × 1½". Fold the 3" edges to the wrong side to meet at the center of the strip. Fold it in half again to enclose the raw edges, and sew a straight stitch along the double-folded edge to make a tail. Fold this in half and insert the two ends into a corner of the edge that is turned and pinned.

9. Sew with a straight stitch across the pinned edge to close.

10. Hand or machine quilt along all seam lines.

To Finish an Apron

4. Cut two strips from the "base" fabric, 3" × 22" (the width of your fabric, cut in half). Fold each in half, lengthwise, with face sides together (Fig. 3-28). Sew a narrow (⅜") seam allowance the length of each strip and across one short end. Turn right side out through the narrow opening and press.

5. Pin or baste the raw edge of the strip to the raw edges at the top corners of one of the finished quilt blocks, ¼" from the sides, and right sides together. Fold the

tie ends neatly and safety pin them to the center of the quilt block to keep them out of the way.

6. Cut three squares each of backing and polyester batting equal to the size of the finished quilt blocks.

7. Place the backing and quilt blocks face sides together, and place a square of polyester batting on top of these. Pin around three sides through all layers, pinning the sides and top edge (the edge with the ties on the bib piece).

8. Sew around these three sides with a ¼" seam allowance, double stitching over the tie ends of the bib. Trim the seams, clip the corners, and turn right side out. Unpin the ties from the face of the bib section.

9. Turn the raw edges ¼" to the inside on the two quilt squares to be used as pockets. Machine topstitch near the edge to close.

10. Machine quilt following the seam lines on all three quilt blocks.

11. Cut a piece of base fabric, 28" × 44" (the width of the fabric) for the skirt. Hem the 28" sides with a narrow double fold. Turn the bottom edge to the wrong side ½", and again 1", and straight stitch by machine across the upper edge of these folds to hem. Press.

12. Measure 8" from the hemmed sides and place the edge of each pocket at this measurement, with the top of the pocket 6" from the top raw edge of the skirt. The topstitched side of the pocket should be at the bottom.

13. Topstitch around the sides and bottom of both pockets, reinforcing the ends of the seams at the top.

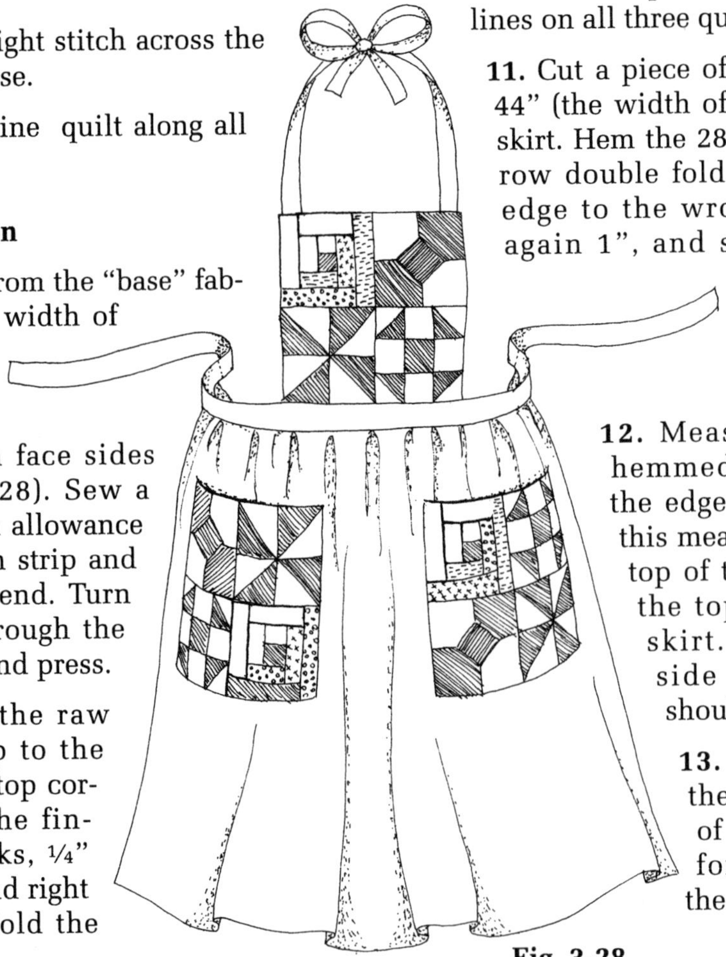

Fig. 3-28

14. Sew a wide basting stitch ¼" from the upper raw edge and pull the thread to gather the skirt evenly to 26" wide.

15. Cut two strips of fabric, 27" × 2½". Sew one edge of one of these strips, right sides and raw edges together, to the gathered edge of the skirt with a ¼" seam allowance. The strip should be ½" longer than the skirt at either end.

16. Center the raw edge of the bib on the opposite side of the same strip and sew it in place with a ¼" seam allowance. Fold the bib and the strip, face sides together, against the skirt along the seam that attached the bib to the skirt.

17. Place the face side of the next strip against the wrong side of the gathered edge of the skirt, with raw edges together, and sew in place with a ¼" seam allowance.

18. Fold the remaining raw edges of the two strips ¼" to the wrong side. Press.

19. Pin these folded edges together evenly. Tuck the seam allowance of the bib to the inside of the strips and pin the edges closed.

20. Topstitch close to the edge across the length of the strips, including the bib section. Fold the raw edges at either side to the inside, but do not stitch closed.

21. Cut a strip of fabric, 7" × 44" (the width of the fabric). Cut it in half to make two 22"-long pieces. Fold these in half lengthwise, right sides and raw edges together.

22. Sew down the long edge and one short side with a ¼" seam allowance on both strips. Clip the corners, turn right sides out, and press.

23. Pleat the remaining raw end on each strip and tuck this end into the open ends of the waistband. Topstitch securely to hold.

To Finish a Place Mat

4. Follow Steps 1–3, but complete 15 assorted 4" quilt blocks for each place mat. Sew these together in rows of five each, to make three rows of five, and sew these rows together to make a rectangle 12½" × 20½".

5. Cut backing and polyester batting equal size to your finished rectangle.

6. Complete Steps 5–10 of How to Finish a Potholder, omitting Step 8.

4

The Bathroom

A friend once said to me, "Only a quilting fanatic would think of a way to put quilts in the bathroom!" Perhaps these accessories don't fit the true definition of a quilt, but you have to admit quilt-look accessories add charm and ambiance to any room. And if glamorous boutiques and catalogs can offer imported accessories like these at astronomical prices, why couldn't you have the same expensive looks in your bath, with the pride and satisfaction that comes from hand-crafting them yourself at a fraction of the price?

Flower Basket Accessories

These bright and beautiful baskets are actually 12" quilt blocks (see color Fig. 13). You can substitute any 12" quilt block pattern to create an endless variety of decorating possibilities. I've chosen to use 4" basket blocks to add variety and eye appeal, although any 4¾" (with ⅜" seam allowance included) pieced or plain square of fabric could be substituted.

Shower Curtain, Sink Skirt, and Toilet-Lid Cover

Because the basket blocks are constructed in the same way for all projects, I've simplified the directions by combining portions of instructions for the shower curtain, sink skirt, and toilet-lid cover. Instructions are written generically for completing the basket blocks for each of these projects, with specific figures given in parentheses in each step, for each individual project.

Steps 1–15: Get started on your shower curtain, sink skirt, or toilet-lid cover

Steps 16–26: Continue your shower curtain or sink skirt

Steps 27–34: Complete your shower curtain

Steps 35–43: Complete your sink skirt

Steps 44–59: Complete your toilet-lid cover

Flower Basket Shower Curtain Materials Required

4 yards white or other background fabric

1¼ yards fabric for the large baskets

½ yard fabric for the small baskets

2¼ yards fabric for the border strips

4¼ yards backing fabric or 2⅛ yards 90" sheeting

2 yards paper-backed fusible web

Thread (for appliqué and for sewing the pieces together)

Tracing or other paper for transferring the handle pattern

Before cutting any fabric for your shower curtain, cut six strips from the background fabric, each 2¾" × 80". Set these aside for later use. See cutting diagrams, Figs. 4-1 through 4-11.

Background fabric　　　　Fold

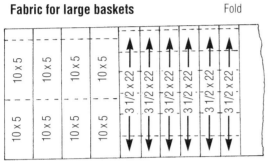
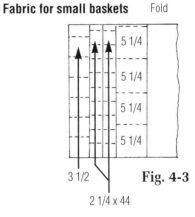

2 3/4 x 80

13 3/4 x 13 3/4　13 1/4 (2)　13 1/4 (2)　13 1/4 (2)　13 1/4 (2)　13 1/4 (2)

3 1/2 x 40　3 1/2 x 40　3 1/2 x 40

9 1/2 x 3　9 1/2 x 3　9 1/2 x 3　9 1/2 x 3　9 1/2 x 3　9 1/2 x 3　9 1/2 x 3　9 1/2 x 3

3　3　3　3　3　3　3

5 1/2　5 1/2　5 1/2　5 1/2

3 1/4　2 1/4　1 3/4

Fig. 4-1

Fabric for large baskets　　Fold

10 x 5　10 x 5　10 x 5　10 x 5

10 x 5　10 x 5　10 x 5　10 x 5

3 1/2 x 22　3 1/2 x 22　3 1/2 x 22　3 1/2 x 22　3 1/2 x 22　3 1/2 x 22

Fig. 4-2

Fabric for small baskets　　Fold

5 1/4　5 1/4　5 1/4　5 1/4

3 1/2

2 1/4 x 44

Fig. 4-3

Border fabric　　　　Fold

1 3/4 x 80

4 x 76

4 x 76

Fig. 4-4

Background fabric　　　　Fold

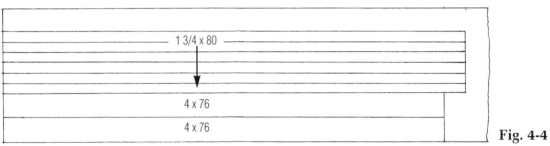

2 3/4 x 54

2 3/4 x 54

9 1/2 x 3　9 1/2 x 3　9 1/2 x 3　9 1/2 x 3　3　3

13 3/4

3 1/4　2 1/4 x 10

13 1/4　13 1/4　5 1/2　1 3/4 x 15

3 1/2 x 37

Fig. 4-5

Fabric for large baskets　　Fold

10 x 5

10 x 5

3 1/4 x 20　3 1/4 x 20

Fig. 4-6

Fabric for small baskets　　Fold

5 1/4

5 1/4

5 1/4

5 1/4

2 1/4 x 14

Fig. 4-7

Border fabric　　　　Fold

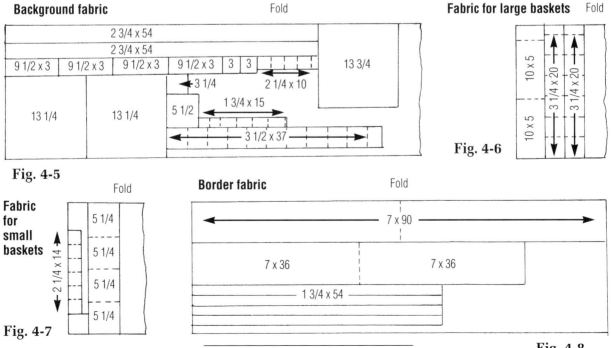

7 x 90

7 x 36　　7 x 36

1 3/4 x 54

Fig. 4-8

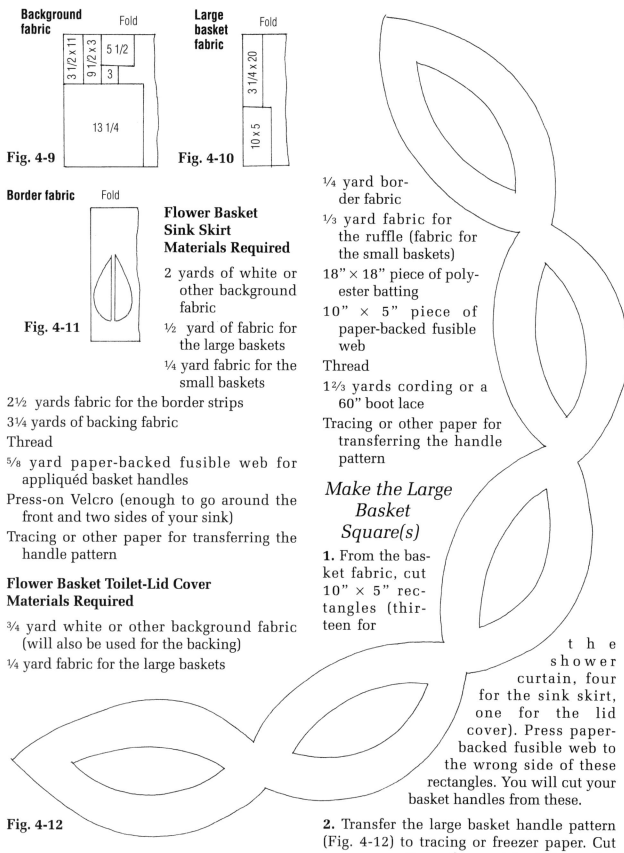

Background fabric

Fold

3 1/2 x 11

9 1/2 x 3

5 1/2

3

13 1/4

Fig. 4-9

Large basket fabric

Fold

3 1/4 x 20

10 x 5

Fig. 4-10

Border fabric

Fold

Fig. 4-11

Flower Basket Sink Skirt Materials Required

2 yards of white or other background fabric

½ yard of fabric for the large baskets

¼ yard fabric for the small baskets

2½ yards fabric for the border strips

3¼ yards of backing fabric

Thread

⅝ yard paper-backed fusible web for appliquéd basket handles

Press-on Velcro (enough to go around the front and two sides of your sink)

Tracing or other paper for transferring the handle pattern

Flower Basket Toilet-Lid Cover Materials Required

¾ yard white or other background fabric (will also be used for the backing)

¼ yard fabric for the large baskets

¼ yard border fabric

⅓ yard fabric for the ruffle (fabric for the small baskets)

18" × 18" piece of polyester batting

10" × 5" piece of paper-backed fusible web

Thread

1⅔ yards cording or a 60" boot lace

Tracing or other paper for transferring the handle pattern

Make the Large Basket Square(s)

1. From the basket fabric, cut 10" × 5" rectangles (thirteen for the shower curtain, four for the sink skirt, one for the lid cover). Press paper-backed fusible web to the wrong side of these rectangles. You will cut your basket handles from these.

2. Transfer the large basket handle pattern (Fig. 4-12) to tracing or freezer paper. Cut out your pattern, then cut basket handles from the prepared rectangles described in Step 1.

Fig. 4-12

3. From your background fabric, cut 13¼" squares (seven for the shower curtain, two for the sink skirt, one for the lid cover). Cut these in half on a diagonal to make triangles. You will have one more than is needed for the shower curtain and lid cover. Use the extra one from the shower curtain for the lid cover or vice versa.

4. Position your basket handles on these triangles, as shown in Fig. 4-13. Pin, press, or glue in place.

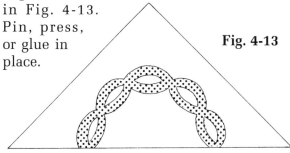

Fig. 4-13

5. Using a thread color that matches your fabric and a closely set zigzag stitch, machine appliqué around the raw edges of the basket handles.

6. Use a rotary cutter and plastic ruler throughout the rest of the project for quick and easy cutting. From the basket fabric, cut strips 3¼" × 22" (twelve for the shower curtain, four for the sink skirt, one for the lid cover). Cut the strips into six 3¼" squares. Stack these squares neatly and cut them in half on a diagonal to make triangles.

7. From your background fabric, cut 3¼"-wide strips, as follows:

Shower curtain: three strips, 40" long
Sink skirt: one strip, 37" long
Lid cover: one strip, 11" long

From these strips, cut 3¼" squares (thirty-three for the shower curtain, ten for the sink skirt, three for the lid cover). Cut these squares in half on a diagonal.

8. Place triangles from your background fabric, face sides together, with triangles of basket fabric. Sew these together on the long side of the triangles, using ³⁄₈" seam allowances, to make five squares for each of the quilt blocks needed for the project you are working on (sixty-five for the shower

curtain, twenty for the sink skirt, five for the lid cover). The quickest method is to sew them together in a long chain, with just a bit of thread between each set, which can be snipped later.

9. From the background fabric, cut rectangles 9¼" × 2¾" (twenty-six for the shower curtain, eight for the sink skirt, two for the lid cover). Place them in twos, face sides and raw edges together, stacking them neatly. Place a mark on the edge of one long side of the top rectangle, 2¾" from the corner. Cut a diagonal line from this mark to the nearest corner on the opposite long edge, through all the rectangles. See Fig. 4-14.

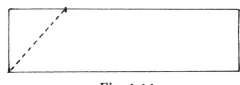

Fig. 4-14

10. Sew a short side of a triangle of the basket fabric to each edge opposite the angled edge of the shapes you just cut, making them parallelograms, each set of two being mirror images.

11. From your background fabric, cut 2¾" squares (thirteen for the shower curtain, four for the sink skirt, one for the lid cover).

12. Align the previously cut triangles, pieced squares, parallelograms, and the squares you just cut as shown in Fig. 4-15. Connect the pieces with a + between them

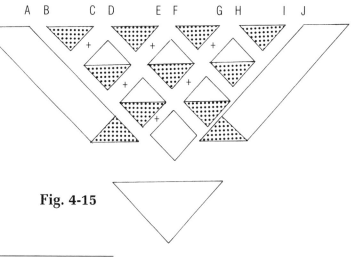

Fig. 4-15

by placing them face sides and raw edges together, and sew each seam with a ⅜" seam allowances.

13. Sew the resulting pieces together as shown in Fig. 4-15, sewing edges A+B, C+D, E+F, G+H, and finally I+J. There will be extra triangles of basket fabric remaining after completing the necessary quilt blocks. You may discard them.

14. From your background fabric, cut 5¼" squares (seven for the shower curtain, two for the sink skirt, one for the lid cover). Cut these in half to become the bottom corner of each basket, by sewing the long edge of this triangle to the long edges of the two lower triangles with a ⅜" seam allowance. See Fig. 4-13. There will be one left for the shower curtain and lid cover.

15. Complete your basket squares by sewing the appliquéd handle half of each square to the pieced basket half, face sides together, along the long edge of each large triangle, using a ⅜" seam allowance (Fig. 4-16).

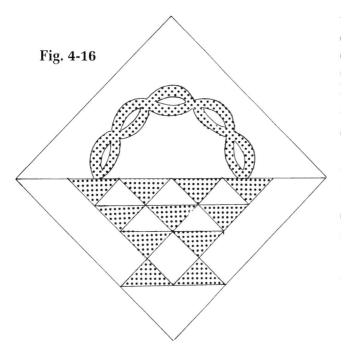

Fig. 4-16

Make the Small Basket Squares

Skip to Step 44 to complete your toilet-lid cover. Steps 16-22 are optional. You may replace these small basket squares with any 4¾" squares of pieced or plain fabric.

Note: Throughout this book, there is a variety of 4" quilt blocks. I have included a ¼" seam allowance for all of these "mini" blocks, except for the small basket block in the Bath chapter. The small basket block uses a ⅜" seam allowance in order to maintain consistency throughout the project. I prefer a ⅜" seam allowance for home-decorating projects because of the added strength, wearability, and washability provided by a slightly wider seam allowance. The smaller, ¼" seam allowance in the "mini" quilt blocks is simply for ease in working with smaller pieces.

16. From your background fabric, cut 3¼" squares (twelve for the shower curtain, two for the sink skirt). Cut them in half on a diagonal to make triangles. These are the large background triangles.

17. From your fabric for the small baskets, cut 3¼" squares (six for the shower curtain, one for the sink skirt). Cut these in half on a diagonal to make triangles. These are the large basket triangles.

18. From your fabric for the small baskets, cut 2¼"-wide strips as follows:

Shower curtain: two strips, 44" long
Sink skirt: one strip, 14" long

Cut 2¼" squares from these strips (thirty-six for the shower curtain, six for the sink skirt).

19. From your background fabric, cut 2¼" wide strips as follows:

Shower curtain: two strips, 28" long
Sink skirt: one strip, 10" long

Cut 2¼" squares from these strips (twenty-four for the shower curtain, four for the sink skirt). Stack all of the squares from Steps 18 and 19 neatly, and cut them in half on the diagonal. These are the small basket and background triangles.

20. From your background fabric, cut 1¾" wide strips as follows:

Shower curtain: two strips, 44" long
Sink skirt: one strip, 15" long

From these strips, cut 1¾" squares and 1¾" × 2 ¾" rectangles as follows:

Shower curtain: twelve squares, twenty-four rectangles
Sink skirt: two squares, four rectangles

21. Place one large basket triangle and one large background triangle, face sides together, and sew with a ⅜" seam allowance along the long edge of the triangles. Repeat this process to complete squares (twelve for the shower curtain, two for the sink skirt). In the same way, sew a small basket triangle to a small background triangle, continuing until you have completed the necessary small squares (48 for he shower curtain, eight for the sink skirt). Stitch these together in a chain as before, and snip between the sets when you are done.

22. Position the remaining pieces as shown in Fig. 4-17. Sew the pieces, face sides and raw edges together, sewing blocks into strips as for the large basket block. Complete your

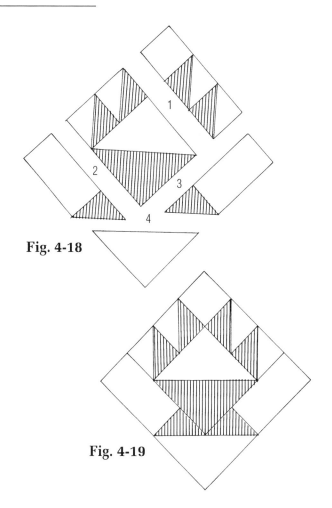

Fig. 4-18

Fig. 4-19

small basket block by sewing the strips together, following the number sequence in Fig. 4-18. A completed block is illustrated in Fig. 4-19. (You will need twelve small basket blocks for the shower curtain, and two for the sink skirt.)

23. From your fabric for the border strips, cut 1¾"-wide strips as follows:

Shower curtain: twelve strips, 80" long (the length of your fabric yardage)
Sink skirt: eight strips, 54" long (1½ yards)

From your background fabric, cut 2¾" wide strips as follows:

Shower curtain: six strips, 80" long
Sink skirt: four strips, 54" long

Sew each strip of background fabric between two strips of border fabric using ⅜" seam allowances. Press the seam allowances

Fig. 4-17

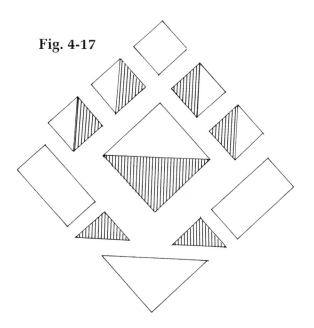

toward the darker fabric. Cut the resulting strips into 12¾" lengths as follows:

Shower curtain: thirty-six strips
Sink skirt: sixteen strips

Each resulting strip should measure 4¾" × 12¾". You may discard any excess left from the long strips.

24. From the fabric for the small baskets, cut 5¼" squares (six for the shower curtain and six for the sink skirt). Stack these neatly and cut them in half on a diagonal to make triangles. These are the small triangles around the outer edge of the pieced portion of your project.

25. From your background fabric, cut 13¼" squares (four for the shower curtain, two for the sink skirt). Cut these in half on a diago-nal to make triangles. These fill in the side edges of your projects.

26. From your background fabric, cut 13¾" squares (one for the shower curtain, two for the sink skirt). Cut these squares into fourths diagonally (in an X) to make the tri-angles for the corners of your projects.

Complete Your Shower Curtain

27. Position all pieces as shown in Fig. 4-20, and sew blocks and strips together diagonal-ly in one direction. Sew the resulting strips together to complete the center of the face of your shower curtain.

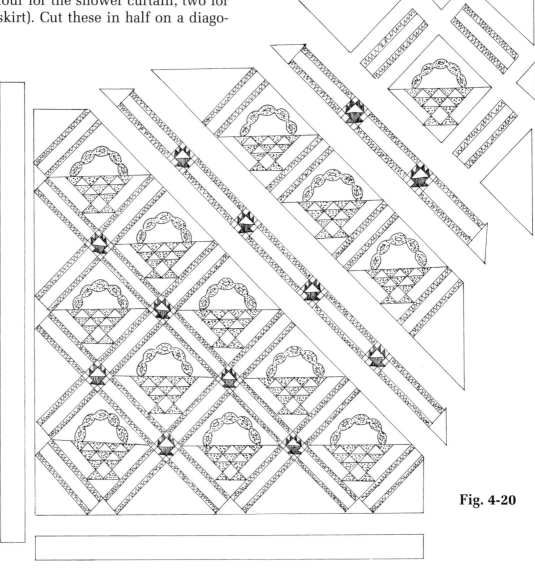

Fig. 4-20

28. From your fabric for the border strips, cut four strips, 76" × 4", and sew them to the sides of this finished center, by pinning one strip to the top and one to the bottom of the project first, sew in place, and cut any excess from each strip. Sew the remaining two strips to the sides in the same manner, including the top and bottom strips already sewn in place. Be careful not to stretch the bias edges of the triangular pieces as you pin the side strips in place. Cut any excess that remains after sewing each strip in place. Press the entire piece.

29. Cut your backing fabric to make two pieces, 76½" long by the width of your fabric, and sew the two pieces, face sides together, down the length of one side edge, to complete your backing. You may substitute 2¼ yards of 90" sheeting.

30. Place the backing, face side up, on a clean floor or a large surface. Put the pieced top of your shower curtain, face side down, centered on the backing. Trim excess backing from all sides and pin the bottom and two sides together.

31. Sew the pinned sides together with a ⅜" seam allowance. Clip the corners and turn face sides out. Pin the face to the backing and sew the layers together by machine quilting through both layers around the large basket blocks. You may add more quilting stitches, if you like, by following all seam allowances in your pieced blocks and borders.

32. Turn the raw edges at the top to the inside, ⅜". To close, pin to hold and topstitch near the fold across the entire edge.

33. Mark the buttonhole positions across this edge by placing marks at either end and marking spaces 6¾" apart between these. There should be a total of twelve buttonholes.

34. By hand or machine, make ½" buttonholes on each mark. Use 18"-long ribbon ties or standard shower curtain rings to display your curtain.

Complete Your Sink Skirt

35. Position two sets of pieces as shown in Fig. 4-21. Sew the pieces together diagonally in one direction, then sew the resulting strips together to finish the pieced portion of your sink skirt.

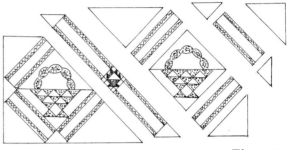

Fig. 4-21

36. Cut two strips of fabric for the border strips, 5" × 90" (the length of your fabric yardage). Cut these in half (45" long) and sew them to the top and bottom edges of each pieced basket section. See Fig. 4-22. Trim excess from the strips and discard.

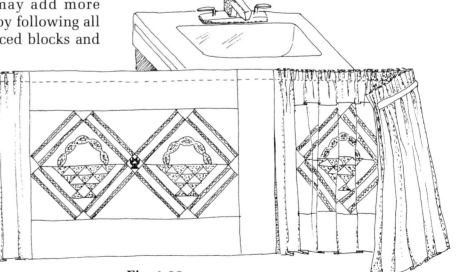

Fig. 4-22

37. Cut four strips of fabric for the border strips, 5" × 36". Sew these to the sides of both pieces, trimming any excess as needed. Press both pieces.

Note: The width of the strips in Steps 36 and 37 can be trimmed or adjusted according to the size of your sink.

38. Cut two pieces of backing fabric, 35" × 57". Place these right sides together with the two face pieces, and pin the top and both side edges.

39. Sew around the pinned top and sides with ⅜" seam allowance. Clip the corners, trim the seam allowances, and turn right sides out. Press the edges to crease them. Insert lightweight polyester batting, if desired.

40. Turn the raw edges at the bottom of both pieces to the inside so that the length of these from top to bottom is equal to the measurement from the top of your sink to the floor. To close, pin and topstitch by machine near the edge. Machine quilt around all seam lines.

41. Sew a basting stitch about 1" from the top edge of both pieces. Machine tack the two pieces together by slightly overlapping them at what will be the front edge, and zigzag with a narrow, closely set stitch, where the basting stitches meet (about 1" from the top).

42. Pull the basting stitches to gather the upper edge evenly, until it is equal to the measurement from wall to wall, around the top edge of the sink (the front and two sides) (Fig. 4-22).

43. Center one half of a strip of Velcro over the gathered basting stitches and sew in place. If using self-stick Velcro, remove the paper backing before sewing it in place. Position the other half of the Velcro strip about ½" from the upper edge of your sink and stick it (or glue it) in place. Fasten the Velcro strips together to hold the skirt in place (Fig. 4-22).

Complete Your Toilet-Lid Cover

44. Measure 1½" from the raw edge of the top and bottom points of your basket square, and mark the measurement. Measure 2" from the raw edge of the corners at either side of the basket, and mark this point as well. Draw a line through each of these marks, evenly "dissecting" the corners from the main square.

45. Trace or reproduce the pattern for the oval borders for the lid cover (Fig. 4-23). Fold your border fabric right sides together and cut two sets of reversed pieces (four pieces total).

46. Place these pieces along the straight sides of your basket square, between the clipped corners. They should form an oval that's longer from top to bottom than from side to side (about 1" longer). Sew these right sides and raw edges together, to the sides of the quilt square.

47. Cut a piece of background (backing) fabric and a piece of polyester batting the same size as the oval. Layer these with the polyester batting between, and the fabric right sides out. Pin or baste to hold the layers together.

48. Machine quilt along the seam lines following the basket motif. Pin the edges of the oval and serge or stitch around the entire piece through all layers.

49. Make the ruffle by cutting two strips of the fabric for the ruffle, 6" × 44" (the width of the fabric). Sew these together into a large circle at the narrow ends, right sides together.

50. Fold the circle of fabric in half lengthwise, wrong sides together, and press to crease the fold. Sew a wide basting stitch about ¼" from the raw edges.

51. Pull the basting stitch to gather it evenly to fit the edges of the quilted lid cover. Pin the edges, right sides and raw edges together, around the entire oval.

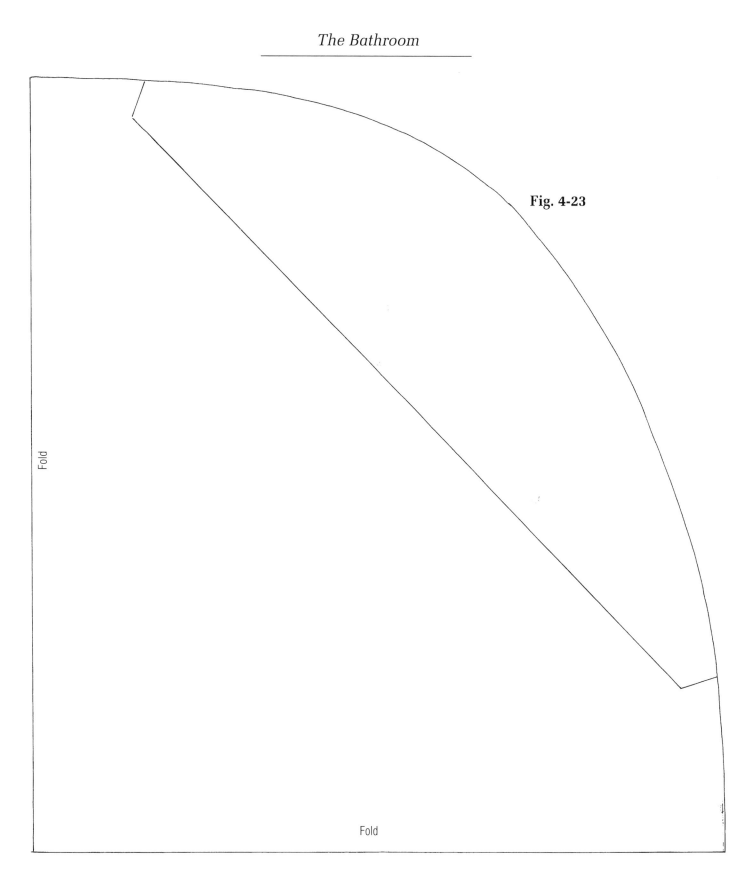

Fig. 4-23

Fold

Fold

52. Sew the ruffle to the quilted lid cover with a ⅜" seam allowance. Trim the seam allowance, and serge or zigzag the seam allowance at the top edge of the block (oval) in a line about 7" long, centered at the top edge.

53. Cut a strip of the background (backing) fabric, 4" × 44". Finish the two narrow ends with a narrow double-folded hem, top-stitched to hold.

54. Form a casing for your cording or boot lace along one long edge by folding the edge ¼" to the wrong side, then again ½". Press the folds.

55. Place the cording inside the folded edge, with about a 10" tail beyond the hemmed narrow end. Sew the casing closed along the fold with a straight stitch, enclosing the cording within it as you sew. The cording should extend beyond the casing at both ends.

56. Run a wide basting stitch about ⅜" from the remaining raw edge of the strip and pull it gently to give a slight curve to the strip.

57. Find the center of the raw edge of the strip and pin it to the center bottom of the oval (the base of the basket), with the right side of the strip against the wrong side of the ruffle, raw edges together.

58. Pin the strip around the edges of the oval. It should end with the hemmed narrow ends of the strip slightly overlapping either side of the 7" serged seam allowance, leaving about 6" open between the hemmed ends of the strip. You can pull the basting stitches on the strip slightly to shorten the strip a bit, if necessary.

59. Sew the strip in place with a ⅜" seam allowance, back-tacking at the ends to anchor it. Clip or serge the seam allowance to finish it.

To display this lid cover, hold it in place on top of your toilet lid. Tie the ends of the cording in a bow near the hinge on the underside of the lid, pulling it tightly to gather the strip to the bottom side of the lid.

Toilet-Tank Topper

This lovely little frill would also look great displayed on a wall in your bathroom.

Materials Required

¼ yard fabric for small baskets

¼ yard white or background fabric

¼ yard border fabric

¼ yard fabric for large baskets (in this case, for the ruffle)

7" × 19" polyester batting

Thread

Preparation and Construction

1. Cut three 3¼" squares of background fabric. Cut them again on a diagonal to make six triangles. These are the large background triangles.

2. Cut two 3¼" squares from the fabric for the small baskets, and cut them again on a diagonal to make four triangles (only three will be used). These are the large basket triangles.

3. Cut a strip of fabric for the small baskets, 2¼" × 21". Cut nine 2¼" squares from this strip. Cut a strip of background fabric, 2¼" × 14", and cut six 2¼" squares from this strip. Stack the squares (both fabrics) neatly and cut them in half on the diagonal. These are the small basket and background triangles.

4. Cut a strip of background fabric, 1¾" × 22". From this strip, cut three 1¾" squares and six 2¾" × 1¾" rectangles.

5. Place one large basket triangle and one large background triangle, face sides together, and sew the long edge of the triangles with a ⅜" seam allowance. Repeat this process to complete three squares.

6. In the same way, sew a small basket triangle to a small background triangle, continuing until your have twelve small squares.

7. Position all the remaining pieces as shown in Fig. 4-17. Sew the pieces, face sides and raw edges together, sewing blocks into strips. Sew the strips together, following the number sequence in Fig. 4-18, and complete three blocks. A completed block is illustrated in Fig. 4-19.

8. Cut three 6" squares of fabric for the border. Cut these diagonally both ways (in an X) to make twelve triangles.

9. Sew the long edge of each of these triangles to each side of your finished basket blocks, face sides and raw edges together, with ⅜" seam allowances.

10. Sew the resulting squares together, side by side, with ⅜" seam allowances, to make a rectangle approximately 6½" × 18". Press.

11. From the fabric for the large baskets, cut two strips, 4" × 44" (the width of the fabric). Sew these together at the narrow ends to make a large circle of fabric. Fold the strips in half, lengthwise, wrong sides and raw edges together, and press to crease the fold.

12. Sew a wide basting stitch about ¼" from the raw edges. Pull the thread to gather the fabric to equal the length around the edge of your finished rectangle. Pin the ruffle, right sides and raw edges together, around the edge of the rectangle, and sew in place with a ⅜" seam allowance.

13. Cut a piece of background fabric (to be used as backing) and polyester batting equal to the size of your finished rectangle.

14. Place the backing fabric right sides together on the finished face and place the polyester batting on top of that. Pin through all layers around the edges to hold.

15. Sew around all edges with a ⅜" seam allowance, leaving an opening about 6" wide for turning right side out. Clip the corners, trim the seam allowances, and turn right side out. Hand or machine stitch to close.

16. Machine quilt following the seams that form the basket design.

Boutique Tissue-Box Cover

Use same materials as Tank Topper, except 7" × 32" polyester batting.

Preparation and Construction

1. Cut four 3¼" squares of background fabric. Cut them again on a diagonal to make eight triangles. These are the large background triangles.

2. Cut two 3¼" squares from the fabric for the small baskets, and cut them again on a diagonal to make four triangles. These are the large basket triangles.

3. Cut a strip of fabric for the small baskets, 2¼" × 28". Cut twelve 2¼" squares from this strip. Cut a strip of background fabric, 2¼" × 19", and cut eight 2¼" squares from this strip. Stack the squares (both fabrics) neatly and cut them in half on the diagonal. These are the small basket and background triangles.

4. Cut a strip of background fabric, 1¾" × 30". From this strip, cut four 1¾" squares and eight 2¾" squares.

5. Place together the face sides of one large basket triangle and one large background triangle, and sew with a ⅜" seam allowance along the long edge of the triangles. Repeat this process to complete four squares.

6. In the same way, sew a small basket triangle to a small background triangle, continuing until you have sixteen small squares.

7. Position all the remaining pieces as shown in Fig. 4-17. Sew the pieces, face sides and raw edges together, sewing blocks into strips. Sew the strips together, following the number sequence in Fig. 4-18, and complete four blocks. A completed block is illustrated in Fig. 4-19.

8. Cut four 6" squares of fabric for the border. Cut these diagonally both ways (in an X) to make twelve triangles.

9. Sew the long edge of each of these triangles to each side of your finished basket blocks, face sides and raw edges together, with ⅜" seam allowances.

10. Cut squares of backing fabric and polyester batting the same size as these finished quilt squares. Place together the face sides of the backing and the pieced blocks, and sew them along the bottom edges with ⅜" seam allowances.

11. Turn face sides out and insert the squares of polyester batting. Machine quilt following the basket designs on each block. Sew a narrow seam allowance around the remaining raw edges to hold the layers neatly together.

12. Cut a 6½" square from the fabric for the large baskets, the background (backing) fabric, and the polyester batting.

13. Place the fabrics face sides together on top of the square of polyester batting, with the backing fabric on top. Draw a 2" line in the center of the top fabric. Sew with a straight stitch around this line, as shown in Fig. 4-24. With sharp scissors, cut on the

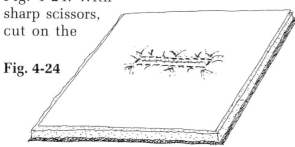

Fig. 4-24

line through all layers. Trim the excess close to the stitching.

14. Lift the backing fabric only and insert its edges through the opening in the center. Pull it through until the layers lie flat, with the polyester batting in between the fabrics, and raw edges together. Sew around the edges with a narrow seam allowance.

15. Sew the top edge of each pieced quilt block to each side of the unpieced square, using ⅜" seam allowances, and leaving ⅜" unsewn at each end of the seams. Finish the raw edges with a serged or zigzag stitched edge.

16. With face sides and raw edges together, sew the side edges of the quilt blocks with ⅜" seam allowances. Start at the bottom, matching the finished edges, and work your way up to the corner, finishing the seam about ⅜" from the end. Serge or zigzag the seam allowances to finish them cleanly.

Seminole Design Shower Curtain and Bath Accessories

Native American influence has made a dramatic impact on decorating. And Seminole patchwork offers an easy way to bring this understated beauty to your home. Brighten your bath in hot-chili-pepper colors, or give it a softer, more traditional look with shades of blush, seafoam, and sand.

If you haven't used a rotary cutter and clear plastic ruler yet, this is the time to try them. Although you can use scissors to cut the strips, you will be amazed at how quickly and easily these strips can be cut with a rotary cutter. No more scissor blisters!

Basic Seminole Patchwork Strips

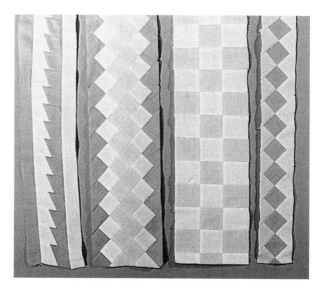

Fig. 4-25

Innumerable design possibilities exist using Seminole patchwork concepts. Once you master the basic designs included here, you can start experimenting with your own combination of shapes, sizes, and colors for custom designing your accessories.

Because there is very little wasted fabric in the Seminole strip-piecing methods, you can decorate your entire bathroom with surprisingly little yardage. The face fabric yardage requirements have been combined for all projects. The individual requirements for each project are listed separately.

Materials Required

Face fabric for all projects: 3 yards each of five solid or mini-print fabric (or a combination of prints and solids)

Thread

Shower Curtain: 4¼ yards of backing fabric or 2⅛ yards of 90" sheeting

Sink Skirt: 3¼ yards of backing fabric; stick-on Velcro (enough to go around the top edge of your sink from wall to wall—measure the front and both sides)

Toilet-Lid Cover: ¾ yard backing fabric; ½ yard polyester batting; 1⅔ yards cording or a 60" boot lace; jumbo cording, optional—1½ yards—if trimming your lid cover with jumbo cording, you will need an additional ¼ yard of one of the fabrics for covering the cord

Tank Topper: ¼ yard each backing fabric polyester batting

Preparation and Construction

Use ¼" seam allowances for all seams in the Seminole strips. The Seminole strips can be sewn into any length required. The finished length of strips for each project should be approximately as follows:

Shower curtain: 75" long

Sink skirt: 58" long

Toilet-lid cover and tank toper: 20" long

Towel trim: measure the width of your towel, plus ½"

1. Fold your assorted fabric in 18" folds so they can be cut the length of the yardage. For ease in handling, you may leave the fabric folded in half widthwise if it has been purchased folded on a bolt rather than rolled on a tube. If doing this, remember that you will be cutting two strips for each lengthwise cut that you make.

2. Cut the selvage evenly from the edge of the fabric. Cut eight 2½-wide strips the length of the fabric (four cuts if your fabric is folded in half widthwise as well as lengthwise).

3. Cut eight 2"-wide strips and four 1½"-wide strips of each color in the same way.

Design 1—Three Colors

4. Label the first three fabric colors you use A, B, and C. Sew a 2" strip of fabric B between 2½" strips of fabrics A and C, using ¼" seam allowances (Fig. 4-26). Repeat this three more times to make four identical sets of strips. Press the seam allowances toward the darker fabrics.

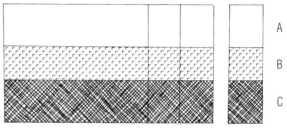

Fig. 4-26

5. Layer these strips, and cut them widthwise (through the seams) with 2" spacing between cuts.

6. Sew the resulting pieces together into strips (Fig. 4-27). Press.

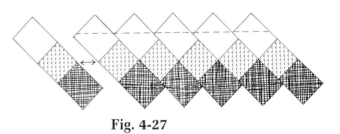

Fig. 4-27

7. Cut off the angled tips of each peak of fabric A and C, as shown in Fig. 4-27.

8. Sew a 2" strip of fabric A and C to opposite sides of the resulting strips (Fig. 4-28).

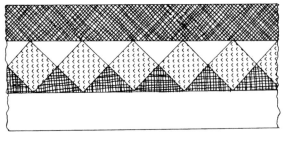

Fig. 4-28

Design 2—Two colors

9. Label the remaining two fabric colors D and E. Sew a 2½" strip of fabric D between two 2½" strips of fabric E using ¼" seam allowances (Fig. 4-29).

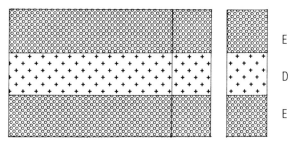

Fig. 4-29

10. Reverse the fabric order and sew 2½" strips of fabric E between 2½" strips of fabric D, again making two sets of strips (Fig. 4-30). Press all seam allowances toward the darker fabric.

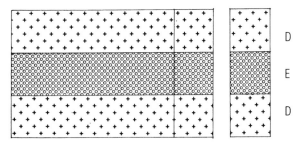

Fig. 4-30

11. Layer the strips and cut them into 2½" segments widthwise (through the seams). Sew the resulting pieces together into a long strip using ¼" seam allowances (Fig. 4-31). Press.

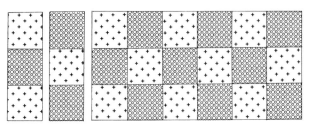

Fig. 4-31

Design 3—Five colors

12. Sew 2"-wide strips of fabrics A, B, C, D, and E together with ¼" seam allowances. Repeat this to make four matching sets.

13. Sew 2½" wide strips of fabric B to opposite sides of each set of strips (Fig. 4-32). Press all seam allowances toward the darker fabrics.

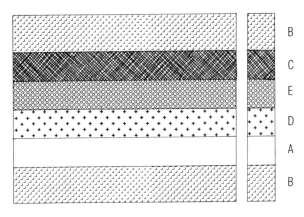

Fig. 4-32

14. Layer the strips and cut them widthwise (through all seams) into 2" segments. Sew the resulting pieces together as shown in Fig. 4-33 using ¼" seam allowances.

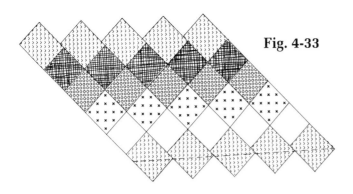

Fig. 4-33

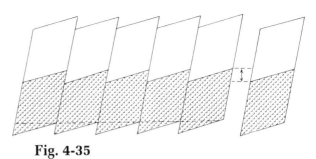

Fig. 4-35

15. Cut off the angled tips of each peak of fabric B on both sides of the strip, as shown in Fig. 4-33.

Design 4—Two colors

16. This design can use any two colors, and strip width, providing the strips are the same width for both colors. Sew the two strips together using a ¼" seam allowance. You should have enough strips left to do various combinations of strips. Press the seam allowances toward the darker fabric.

17. Cut the strips on an angle into segments in widths equal to the cut width of each strip. Using the 60° line on a clear plastic ruler, cut on a diagonal to the nearest opposite corner. If a clear plastic ruler is not available, measure from the corner edge of one strip to a point equal to the cut width of the strips you are using, and cut diagonally as above. See Fig. 4-34.

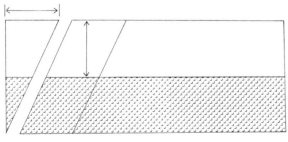

Fig. 4-34

18. Sew the segments together as shown in Fig. 4-35. Press.

19. Cut off the angled tips of each peak evenly on both sides of the strip.

Preparing Your Seminole Fabric for Each Project

20. Sew the finished Seminole strips, long sides together, using any remaining single fabric strips or a combination of solid strips as dividing lines between the pieced strips. You may sew these in any order you choose, using ¼" seam allowances. Sew them to the following sizes for each project:

Shower curtain: 74" × 74"

Sink skirt: two pieces, each 35" × 57"

Toilet-lid cover: 19" × 19"

Tank topper: 8" × 20"

Towel trim: use only one design of Seminole trim for each towel

Press each entire piece after it has been sewn to the size needed.

Finishing Instructions

Shower Curtain: Follow Steps 29–34 of the Flower Basket Shower Curtain.

Sink Skirt: Follow Steps 38–43 of the Flower Basket Sink Skirt.

Toilet-Lid Cover: Follow 8 steps below.

1. Transfer the pattern for the toilet-lid cover (Fig. 4-23), or trace a pattern using your own toilet lid, adding 1" all around.

2. Cut the shape of your toilet lid from the Seminole pieced fabric. Cut backing fabric and polyester batting to the same size.

3. Sandwich the polyester batting between the backing and pieced face fabric, with face sides out. Pin to hold, and machine quilt through the layers, following the seam lines of the Seminole fabric.

4. Pin the outer edges to hold them together and stitch around the entire edge with a narrow seam allowance.

5. Steps 5–7 are optional. Make jumbo cording. Cut two strips of extra fabric, each 4½" × 44" (the width of the fabric). Sew them, face sides and raw edges together, at one of the narrow ends of the strips.

6. Starting at one end of the cording, wrap the strip around it lengthwise, right sides out and raw edges together. Pin or stitch the fabric to the cording at this end to hold them together. Sew the fabric around the cording with a ⅜" seam allowance, or so the fabric is not too tight around the cording. Gather the fabric slightly on the cording by sliding it down with every several inches you stitch.

7. Sew the finished cording around the quilted toilet-lid cover, raw edges together, starting at what will be the hinged end of your lid cover. Leave about 1" unstitched at the start. When you get all the way around, but before you sew the cording down, cut it so it overlaps the starting point by about 1". Pull back the fabric, and cut the cording inside the fabric casing even with the starting point. Fold the fabric ½" to the inside then wrap it around the unstitched begin-

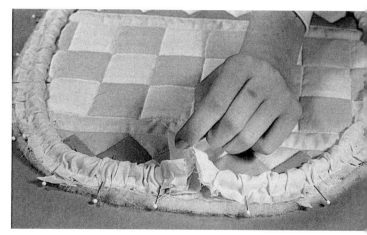

Fig. 4-36

ning of the cording. Stitch through all seam allowances to hold it in place (Fig. 4-36).

8. Continue with Steps 53–59 of the Flower Basket Toilet-Lid Cover.

Towel Trim

1. Use any purchased towel. Cut your trim ½" wider than the towel. Fold all edges of the trim ¼" to the wrong side.

2. Position the trim on your towel, and pin around all edges to hold.

3. Topstitch close to the edges around all sides of your trim.

4. Machine quilt following the seam lines of your Seminole design.

5

Special Touches

Do you love to sew or quilt? Are you a fabriholic, with more assorted fabrics than you can use in a decade? This chapter was written for you.

If you're like me, you can't pass up a fabric sale or a fabulous print without purchasing at least a yard or two. But what do you do with those odd yardages when they're not quite enough to complete a quilt? Make quilted and quilt-look accessories for family, friends, and every room in your home.

Lampshades

Everyone has at least one standard, boring lampshade that could benefit from restyling. Here are four new looks that use the same basic pattern and will certainly "light up" your old lamps.

For lasting quality, don't place lamps with fabric shades in direct sunlight—the shades may become sun-bleached.

Basic Pattern

This pattern is designed to fit any standard lampshade like the ones shown in Figs. 5-1 and 5-2. You may remove the fabric cover which is already on the frame of your shade or leave it on. However, if the

Fig. 5-1

Fig. 5-2

fabric on your current lampshade is textured or patterned, remove it, so it won't detract from your new look when the light is on.

This pattern is simply a "slip cover" for your current lampshade.

Materials Required for Cylindrical Lampshade

Base fabric: To determine yardage, measure around the widest part of your lampshade; add 2" to this measurement; measure from top to bottom, and add 6" to this measurement

Thread

¼" elastic—2 lengths, each 25% shorter than the measurements around the top and bottom rims of your lampshade

Preparation and Construction

1. Cut your base fabric to the measurements described above.

2. Refer to the instructions that follow for the individual designs to appliqué or embellish your base fabric, or use any plain or patterned decorator fabric without added embellishment or with lace trim and fringe.

3. After appliquéing or otherwise decorating your base fabric, fold it in half, face sides together, so the raw side edges meet.

4. Sew the side edges together with a ⅜"
seam allowance, creating a tube to slip over
your lampshade frame. Serge or zigzag the
seam to finish it neatly.

5. Fold the top and bottom raw edges to the
wrong side with a ¼" turn, then fold it again
½" to make a casing for your elastic. You'll
stitch it later.

6. If you haven't already done so, cut two
pieces of ¼"-wide elastic 25% shorter than
the measurements around the top and bottom rims of your shade. Sew the ends of
each piece together to make two circles of
elastic.

7. Sew the elastic inside the folded casing at
either end of your lampshade slipcover,
making sure the smaller circle is at the narrower end.

8. Slide this new cover over your old lampshade frame, adjusting it evenly.

**Materials and Construction for
Conical Shade**

For lampshades having a measurement
around the top which is more than 3" smaller than the measurement around the bottom
of the shade, make a pattern and purchase
fabric to fit your pattern.

1. Place two straight pins, directly above
and below each other, one on each rim.

2. With the old fabric still on your shade,
rub chalk around the top
and bottom rims or use
a fabric marker to mark
your pattern as you
roll the shade over a
large piece of tissue
paper, other paper, or
inexpensive fabric
(Fig. 5-3).

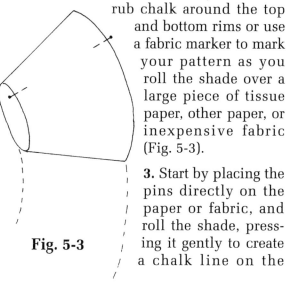

Fig. 5-3

3. Start by placing the
pins directly on the
paper or fabric, and
roll the shade, press-
ing it gently to create
a chalk line on the
paper or fabric. Or follow the rim of the
shade (top and bottom) using a pencil or
fabric marker to mark the paper or fabric.
Continue pinning all the way around.

4. Measure each line, then measure around
the top and bottom rims of your shade to be
sure the measurements are the same.

5. Add 2" to the length of each curved line
of your pattern, then connect the ends of the
curved lines with straight lines.

6. Continue the straight lines 3" above and
below the curved chalk lines, and redraw
the curves evenly above and below the original lines to connect the straight lines (Fig. 5-
4). Use this as the pattern for your base fabric. Complete your shade as described in
Steps 2–8 for the cylindrical shade.

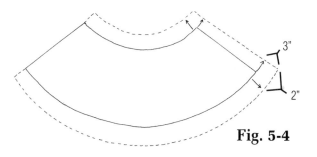

Fig. 5-4

Pennsylvania Dutch
Appliqué

This simple design is displayed to its
best advantage when machine appliquéd on
good-quality cotton or poly-cotton broad-
cloth-type fabric (color Fig. 5). If you use a
heavy duty iron-on craft interfacing, like
craft-weight Heat N Bond, you can simply
press-and-go, without any machine
appliquéing.

Additional Materials Required

Assorted fabrics for appliqué pieces

Paper-backed fusible web

Thread to match your assorted fabrics, for
machine appliqué

Tracing or freezer paper for transferring your
appliqué pattern

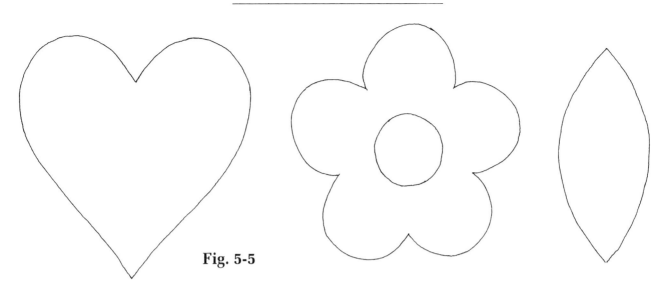

Fig. 5-5

Apply Design to Base Fabric

Refer to the Basic Pattern for measuring instructions.

1. Trace or transfer the appliqué designs shown in Fig. 5-5. Press paper-backed fusible web to the wrong side of your assorted fabrics. Cut out the required pieces using the patterns.

Fig. 5-7

Fig. 5-6

2. Using a large dinner plate, draw a circle in the center of your base fabric. Arrange your cut fabric pieces around the circle, as shown in Fig. 5-6. Pin, press, or glue in place.

3. If desired, machine appliqué around the edges of these fabrics using a narrow, closely set zigzag stitch. In the same way, machine stitch the circle drawn on your fabric. You can also arrange these pattern pieces as shown in Fig. 5-7.

4. Finish your lampshade as described in the Basic Pattern.

Hawaiian-Style "Cutout"

Refer to the Basic Pattern for general information before beginning.

This beautiful design is reminiscent of childhood paper-folding and -cutting projects. Use good-quality cotton or poly-cotton fabrics for the base and cutout fabrics as described in Method 1 below, or translucent cotton voile for the base fabric as described in Method 2 on page 79.

Additional Materials Required

Extra face fabric (per Method 1 or 2, as desired)

Paper-backed fusible web, cut the same size as your extra face fabric

Thread for machine appliqué (optional) and for finishing your lampshade

Optional: Tracing or freezer paper for transferring the patterns

Preparation and Construction, Method 1

1. Press paper-backed fusible web to a 10"–16" piece of face fabric (depending on the size of your shade), and cut it into a square or circle. Remove the paper backing, and fold this piece into quarters.

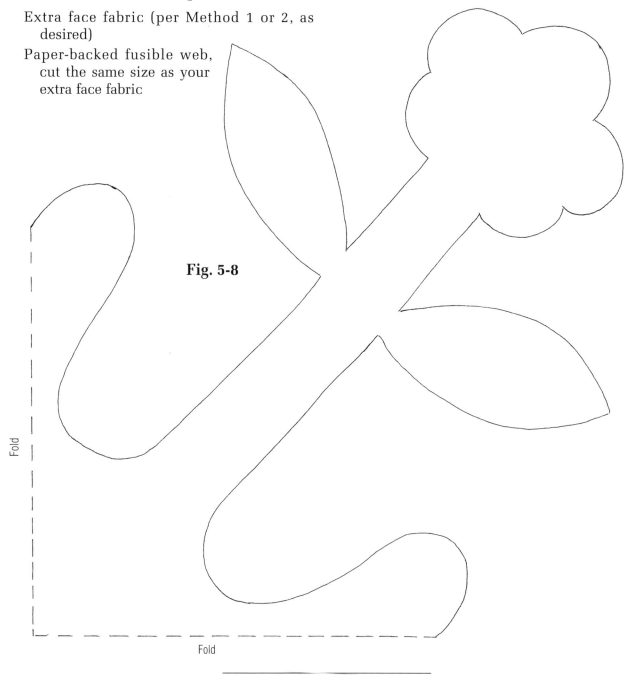

Fig. 5-8

Fold

Fold

2. Use the patterns shown in Figs. 5-8 through 5-10, or create your own designs, drawing them onto the top layer of the fused and folded fabric.

3. Cut out the shapes, and press the cutout fabric in place on your base fabric. Machine appliqué around the edges with a narrow zigzag stitch, or leave it unstitched for a simple, elegant look.

4. Finish as described in the Basic Pattern.

Preparation and Construction, Method 2

1. Fuse paper-backed fusible web to a good-quality cotton or poly-cotton fabric which has been cut to the same size as your base fabric.

2. Remove the paper backing, and fold and cut this prepared piece as desired, with the overall size the same as the base fabric.

3. Press it to a base fabric of translucent cotton voile and machine appliqué, as desired.

4. Finish as described in the Basic Pattern. Your room will glow.

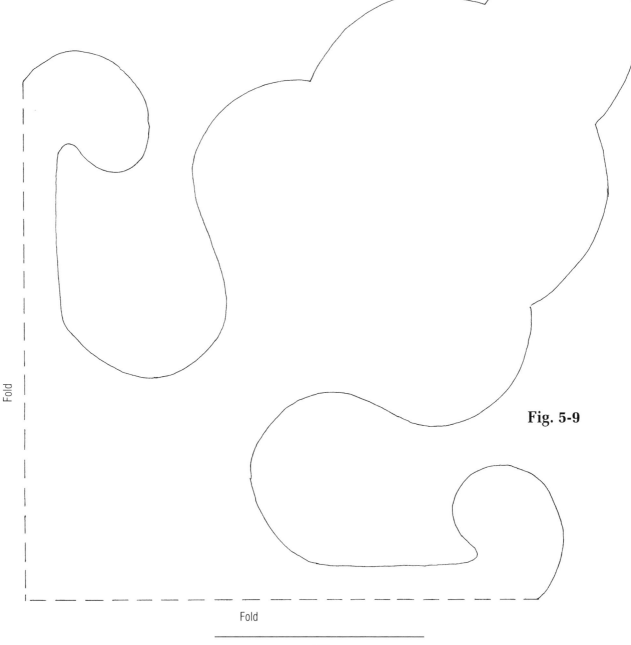

Fig. 5-9

Fold

Fold

Fold

Fig. 5-10

Fold

"Stained Glass" Shade

Visitors to your home will be in awe of the beautiful stained glass looks you create with fabric (color Fig. 1). The basic instructions used for making this design can be used for designing your own stained glass originals. This lampshade is simpler to make than it looks.

Materials Required

½ yard each of assorted appliqué fabrics

Ivory or other pastel fabric to use as your base fabric

1–2 yards of paper backed fusible web

Black or charcoal thread, or one yard of black fabric

which has been fused with paper-backed fusible web, then bias cut in ¼"-wide strips

Tracing or freezer paper for transferring the pattern

Preparation and Construction

Refer to the Basic Pattern for measuring and cutting your base fabric.

1. Use Fig. 5-11 as the basis for the flowers and leaves on the lampshade. The solid lines in the flower can be used alone for the small flower pattern. Add the dashed-line area for the large flower. Transfer the patterns to tracing or freezer paper. For easier cutting, use freezer paper—it can be pressed to your fabric without leaving a residue.

2. Press paper-backed fusible web to the wrong side of your assorted fabrics. Using the patterns, cut pieces from these fabrics about ⅛" larger all around than the pattern itself, so they will slightly overlap when arranged on your base fabric.

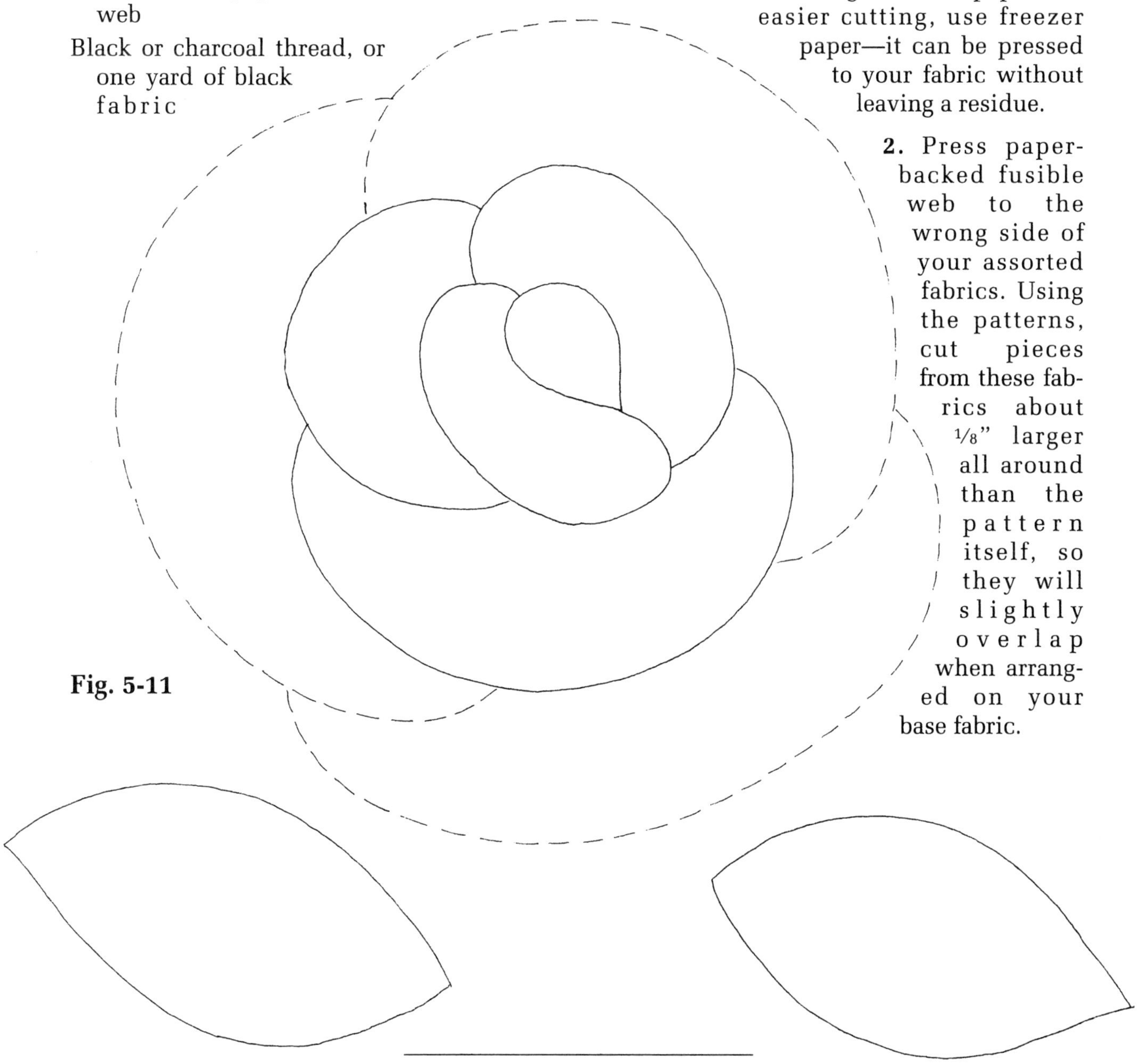

Fig. 5-11

3. Remove the paper backing from the fusible web and arrange the flowers and leaves on your base fabrics, as desired, or as shown in color Fig. 1. Be sure your arrangement is at least 3" from the top and bottom edges. Press the pieces in place.

4. Draw lines on the remainder of your base fabric to mimic leaded glass. You can evenly space the lines in square or rectangular grids, or design your own geometric pattern.

5. Create the "leaded" lines in one of two ways: A. Using black or charcoal thread, machine stitch with a narrow, closely set zigzag setting around all raw edges and on all lines. B. Press paper-backed fusible web to the wrong side of one yard of black fabric. Cut the prepared fabric on a bias into ¼"-wide strips. Remove the paper backing and carefully press the strips over the raw edges of the cut fabric pieces and on all lines, cutting the strips to the length you need as you press them in place.

6. Finish your lampshade as described in the Basic Pattern.

Victorian Crazy Quilt Shade

This super-simple shade (Fig. 5-12) requires almost no sewing at all. It's the perfect solution for using up scraps of fabric and bits of trim. It has an elegant, delicate look when done in assorted white eyelet and lacy fabrics.

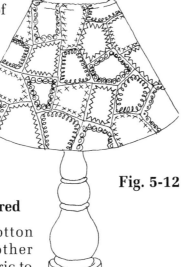

Fig. 5-12

Materials Required

Translucent cotton voile or other semisheer fabric to use as your base fabric (not too delicate)

Assorted fabrics for the patchwork

Paper-backed fusible web

Thread and ¼" elastic as described in the Basic Pattern

Hot or low-melt glue gun

Preparation and Construction

Refer to the Basic Pattern for instructions on measuring and cutting your base fabric.

1. Press paper-backed fusible web to the wrong sides of your assorted fabrics.

2. Cut fabric pieces in assorted shapes from these fabrics. Remove the paper backing and lay the pieces on your base fabric as desired. Trim the edges of the assorted shapes so they only slightly overlap each other. If you don't trim, you will see the excess under the fabrics when the light is turned on.

3. Press the assorted fabric shapes to the base fabric. Be sure to cover the entire base fabric.

4. Add assorted trims and laces around the edges of the various shapes by machine stitching or gluing them in place with a glue gun.

5. Finish your lampshade as described in the Basic Pattern.

Hawaiian Quilt Accessories

Hawaiian quilting is known for its intricate, lacy cutouts of fabric-on-fabric. Hand-stitched Hawaiian-style appliqués are beautiful and delicate. These machine-stitched versions mimic beautiful brocade fabrics, yet are completely machine washable when made with washable fabrics. Use the patterns given here or create your own variations.

The basic instructions are child's play, and if you use a heavy-duty or craft-weight fusible web, you can eliminate the machine appliqué altogether.

Table Topper, Doilies, Chair Protectors, and Coasters

Materials Required

Appliquéd face, each project: two different fabrics of the same weight and fiber content

Backing fabric and polyester batting, cut to the same size as the face fabrics

Paper-backed lightweight fusing web for machine appliquéing the raw edges of your cutout face fabric, or craft-weight fusing web for a non-appliquéd finish

Thread for appliqué, quilting, and finishing

Optional: Double-fold bias tape, lace, fringe, or ruffled trim—enough to go around the outer edges of your project

Preparation and Construction

1. Cut all fabrics, polyester batting, and fusing web to the same size for each project, as follows:

Table topper: 36" square

Doilies and chair protectors: 14" squares or circles; 12" × 16" ovals or rectangles

Coasters: 4¾" squares or circles

2. Press the fusing web to the wrong side of the face fabric that will be "cutout."

3. Remove the paper backing, and fold the fused fabric into quarters. Use the patterns shown in Figs. 5-8 to 5-10 and 5-13 to 5-15, or create your own designs, and draw them onto the top layer of your folded fabric. Cut out the shapes through all layers.

4. Press the cutout face fabric to a base fabric. Machine appliqué around all raw edges of the cutout fabric, as desired.

5. Sew lace, ruffle, or fringe trim, face sides and raw edges together, around all sides of your appliquéd face, as desired, or refer to Step 10, for finishing your project with bias tape.

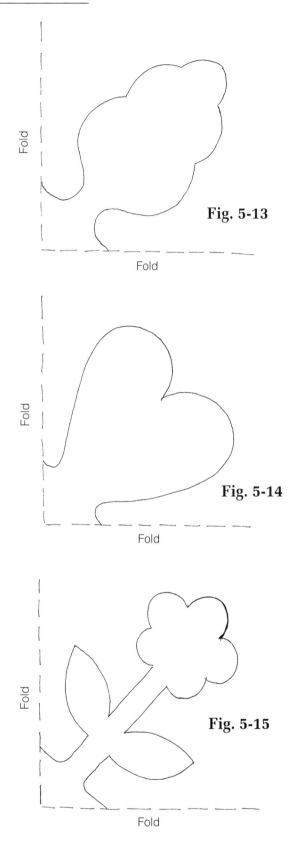

Fig. 5-13

Fig. 5-14

Fig. 5-15

6. Place backing fabric face sides together on your face fabric. Place the polyester batting on top of these and pin around all sides to hold them in place.

7. Sew around all sides with a ⅜" seam allowance: on one side, leave an opening large enough to turn your project face sides out.

8. Clip corners, trim the seam allowances, and turn your project face sides out. Finish the opening by turning the raw edges to the inside, and hand stitch or machine topstitch to close.

9. Machine quilt by following all appliqué seam lines.

10. If you plan to finish the edges of your project with bias tape, sandwich the polyester batting between the appliquéd face and backing fabrics, with right sides facing out. Pin around the edges to hold them together and stitch close to the edges with a narrow seam allowance.

11. Apply double-fold bias tape by pinning it around the raw edges of your project, and stitching it in place, carefully easing around the corners as you go.

12. Overlap the last end of the bias tape over the starting point, folding the raw end underneath. Stitch to hold.

13. Machine quilt around all appliqué seam lines.

"Stained Glass" Accessories

These accessories combine the patterns used for the Stained Glass Lampshade with the instructions for making the Hawaiian Quilt Accessories.

Table Topper, Doilies, Chair Protectors, and Coasters

You will need the same basic materials as described for the Stained Glass Lampshade, plus polyester batting. Refer to Step 1 of the Hawaiian Quilt Accessories for base fabric, backing and polyester batting requirements.

Preparation and Construction

1. Follow Steps 1–5 of the Stained Glass Lampshade, arranging the appliqué pieces on base fabric cut to the sizes described in Step 1 of the Hawaiian Quilt Accessories.

2. Finish your Stained Glass Accessories as described in Steps 5–13 of the Hawaiian Quilt Accessories.

And Sew On...

Patchwork Quilted One-Piece Rocker/Chair Cushion

This unique seat-and-back cushion (color Fig. 7) combines four 16" blocks in one strip. Use the quilt block pattern shown here, or combine any four 16" quilt blocks for your own special look. The overall finished size of this cushion is about 15" × 60".

Material Required

2 yards of Fabric 1 (for one set of points on the star and for the ruffle)

2⅛ yards of Fabric 2 (the other set of points on the star, the backing, and the ties)

⅝ yard of Fabric 3 (the corners and outer edges of the quilt block)

2 yards of a cotton or poly-cotton inexpensive fabric to use as a lining fabric

1 yard extra-loft polyester batting (at least 64" wide)

Thread

5' (60") of 1½" foam cushioning or extra polyester batting

Velcro (optional)

Preparation and Construction

1. From Fabric 3, cut two 4¾"-wide strips, the width of the fabric (44"). From these strips, cut sixteen 4¾" squares. These are the corner squares for each of four blocks (Fig. 5-16).

Fig. 5-16

2. Also from Fabric 3, cut two 5⅜"-wide strips, the width of the fabric. Cut sixteen 5⅜" squares from these strips. Stack these 5⅜" squares neatly and cut them in half on a diagonal to make triangles.

3. Repeat Step 2 for each of Fabrics 1 and 2 (Fig. 5-17).

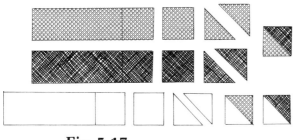

Fig. 5-17

For a quick and easy method of sewing the triangles into squares, Nancy Zieman of Nancy's Notions suggest using the Quick Quarter, available in her catalog. You simply place the larger squares face sides together, and place the Quick Quarter diagonally on top of them. With a chalk pencil or fabric marker, mark the slashed line down the center of the Quick Quarter. Then draw a straight line on either side of the Quick Quarter.

To obtain the necessary ⅜" seam allowances for this project, stitch ⅛" to the outside edge of the straight lines, as shown in Fig. 5-18. Cut the square in half along the slashed line.

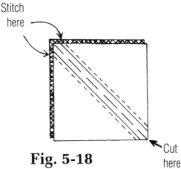

Stitch here

Cut here

Fig. 5-18

For each block for this project, you will need two sets each of face-to-face squares, as follows: Fabrics 1 and 2, Fabrics 1 and 3, and Fabrics 2 and 3.

4. Arrange the pieces as shown in Fig. 5-19. Using ⅜" seam allowances, sew the long edges of the triangles together, face sides and raw edges matching, to make sixteen squares for each block. Press seam allowances toward the darker fabric as you go.

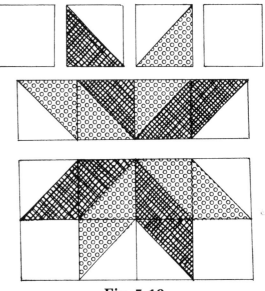

Fig. 5-19

5. Sew the squares together in rows, using ⅜" seam allowances, then sew the rows together to complete the 16" quilt block.

6. Sew the blocks together, end-to-end, to make a strip of four quilt blocks. Press.

7. Cut two pieces of polyester batting and two pieces of the lining fabric equal to the size of the row of quilt blocks. Also cut a piece of Fabric 2 the same size to use as your backing.

8. Separately layer backing (Fabric 2)/polyester batting/lining and pieced-quilt blocks/polyester batting/lining, with polyester batting in between the fabrics, which are face sides out. Pin through all layers on each set and machine quilt following the patchwork seams on the face side, and in a wide grid pattern on the backing.

9. Make the ruffle: Cut seven strips of Fabric 1, 7" wide by the width of the fabric. Sew these strips end-to-end, right sides and raw edges together, to make a large circle of fabric. Fold the strips in half lengthwise, wrong sides together, and press to crease the fold. Sew a wide basting stitch ¼" from the raw edges.

10. Divide the circle into quarters, placing a straight pin at each quarter mark.

11. Pin each quarter mark of your circle of strips to the center of each side of your quilted strip of blocks.

12. Pull the basting stitches to gather the circle of strips evenly into a ruffle. Pin the raw edges of the ruffle to the raw edges of the quilt blocks. Sew the ruffle to the quilt blocks around all raw edges.

13. Cut four strips of Fabric 2, 5" × 65". These are the ties. Hem around all sides of these strips with a narrow double fold to the wrong side, or use a roll-hem foot. Fold these in half, pleat them at the fold, and pin them to the quilted and ruffled face as shown in Fig. 5-20. Machine tack them securely near the fold. Fold the strips neatly and safety pin them to the center of your quilt blocks to keep them out of the way.

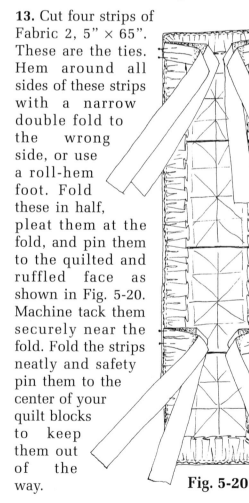

Fig. 5-20

14. Place the quilted backing face side together against the ruffled and quilted face. Pin the long sides together.

15. Sew down both long sides with ⅜" seam allowances, starting and ending about 2" from each corner on the short sides. Turn the entire strip face sides out.

16. Machine stitch through all layers along the seam that divides the seat area from the back (separating the seat quilt block from the three back quilt blocks).

17. Cut a piece of 1½" thick foam into a square about 2" smaller than your seat section, or fold layers of extra polyester batting to approximately the same size. Insert this into the seat section (Fig. 5-21).

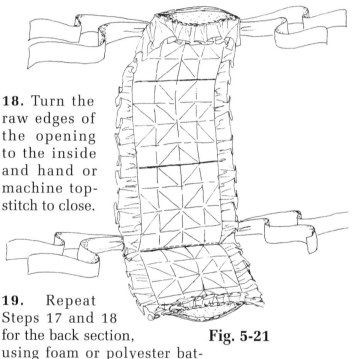

18. Turn the raw edges of the opening to the inside and hand or machine topstitch to close.

19. Repeat Steps 17 and 18 for the back section, **Fig. 5-21** using foam or polyester batting to fit. For a less plump look, leave the back section as is. Finish as described in Step 18. For easy removal of your foam insert, stitch Velcro to the seam allowances.

20. To display this cushion, tie the seat ties to the back rungs of your rocker at the base (seat). Fold the long seat back over the top of your rocker, and wrap the tie ends around the outer rungs. See Fig. 5-22.

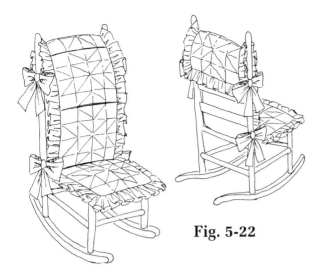

Fig. 5-22

Star Wall Hanging or Crib Quilt

This quick and easy project is made using the same 16" star quilt blocks as used in the Patchwork Quilted One-Piece Rocker Cushion. You can substitute any 16" quilt blocks for your own special look. The finished size of this project is approximately 40" × 50".

Materials Required

1¼ yards of Fabric 1 (for one set of points on the star and the borders on the face on the quilt)

1¾ yards of Fabric 2 (the other set of points on the star and the backing of the quilt)

⅝ yard of Fabric 3 (the corners and outer edges of the quilt blocks)

Polyester batting to fit 42" × 52"

Thread

Preparation and Construction

1. Follow Steps 1–5 of the Patchwork Quilted One-Piece Rocker Cushion to complete four quilt blocks.

2. Sew two sets of two blocks together, face sides and raw edges matching, along one seam, using ⅜" seam allowances.

3. Sew these sets, face sides and raw edges together, along on long seam to complete a large square (Fig. 5-23). Press.

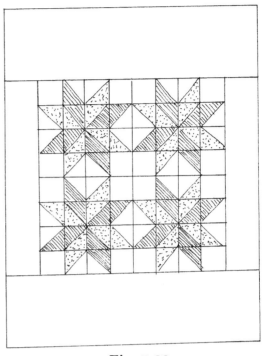

Fig. 5-23

4. From Fabric 1, cut two strips, 5" × 33", cutting the strips from the width of the fabric. Sew these to the side edges of your square of quilt blocks, face sides and raw edges together, using ⅜" seam allowances.

5. Also, from Fabric 1, cut two strips, 10" × 42", and sew these in the same way to the top and bottom edges of your quilt blocks, including the strips already sewn in place. Press the entire piece.

6. Cut backing (from Fabric 2) and polyester batting equal in size to the finished quilt top.

7. Place your quilt top and backing face sides and raw edges together on a large surface. Lay your polyester batting on top of these and pin together the two long sides and one short side through all layers.

8. Sew these sides together through all layers using a ⅜" seam allowance, removing the pins as you sew.

9. Clip the corners, trim the seam allowances, and turn the quilt so the fabrics are face sides out.

10. Turn the remaining raw edges ⅜" to the inside, pinning to hold them in place To hang your quilt from a dowel rod, evenly insert fabric loops into the turned edges and topstitch by machine to close the seam.

11. Pin the face of the quilt through all layers to keep them from shifting. Machine quilt following the seam lines around the quilt blocks and around the border to finish your quilt.

Decorating with 4" Quilt Blocks

Have you ever heard (or said), "I'd love to quilt but don't have the time?" Many people are afraid to start a quilting project for fear that it will take too long to finish and they will lose the motivation to complete it. Don't let such worries keep you from discovering the joy of creative quilting.

These little quilt blocks are perfect for those who don't have a lot of time to really concentrate on a large project. Take a few minutes to cut several blocks from the patterns provided, then sew one or two each day. Before you know it, you will have a room full of quilted accents.

Follow the directions shown with each pattern for cutting and finishing each 4" quilt block. Seam allowances of ¼" have already been included in these little block patterns. Refer to previous chapters for more quilt block patterns.

Materials Required

Assorted bits and pieces of coordinating face fabrics for each quilt block

4½" squares of backing and polyester batting

Thread

Tracing paper for transferring your pattern

Additional materials given with individual projects

Preparation and Construction

Finish the face of your quilt block according to the directions shown with the pattern desired (Figs. 5-24 through 5-26). Press seam allowances toward the darker fabric as you work.

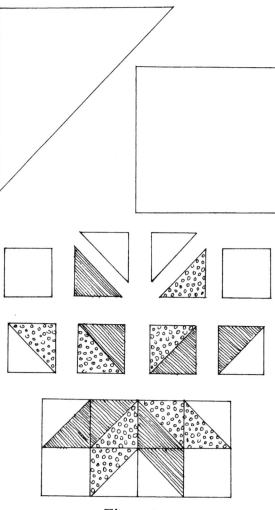

Fig. 5-24

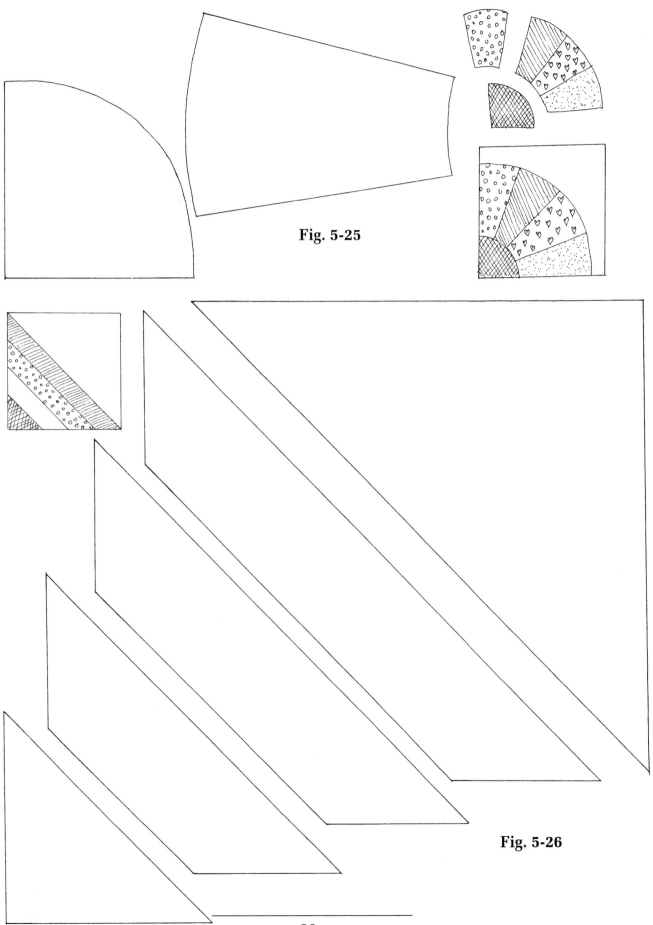

Fig. 5-25

Fig. 5-26

Coasters and Ornaments

No additional materials are necessary.

1. Place the backing fabric face sides together with the finished quilt face. Place the polyester batting on these and pin the edges together through all layers.

2. Sew these together on three sides using ¼" seam allowances. Clip the corners, trim excess from the seam allowances, and turn face sides out.

3. Turn the remaining raw edges ¼" to the inside. For the ornaments only, add a small loop of ribbon or fabric at one corner, as desired, for hanging. Hand or machine stitch to close.

4. Hand or machine quilt, as desired, following the seam lines of your quilt block.

Little Square Anywhere

This fun accent (Fig. 5-27) goes just about anywhere your imagination will allow. Ribbon ties attached to the sides or corners of your individual 4" quilt blocks can be tied or adjusted for a variety of uses.

Cut two 12" (or longer) lengths of ⅜"- to ½"-wide ribbon. Fold one end on each length of ribbon ½" and place the folded end at

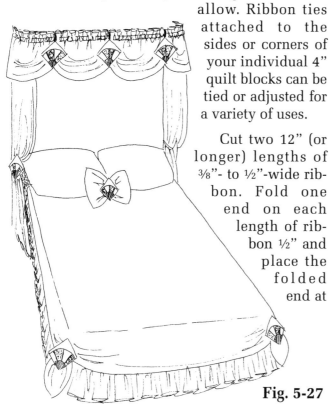

Fig. 5-27

opposite sides or corners of your finished quilt block. Tack them by hand or machine on the back side. Hot glue or hand tack a

loop of elastic to the center of the back of your quilt blocks and you'll have more ways to use and display the little squares.

Here are just a few ideas for your Little Square Anywhere:

Make napkin rings
Hug a corner of your quilt, comforter, or tablecloth
Tie back a curtain
"Butterfly" a pillow
Make a garland
Wrap a roll of toilet tissue
"Pouf" a plain valance
Wrap a gift bag, bottle or box

Quilt Blocks Bell Pull

This decorative accent (Fig. 5-28) is perfect displayed on a door or small wall. You will need three to six finished 4" quilt blocks, as desired, for this project. Refer to the directions shown with each pattern for completing your blocks.

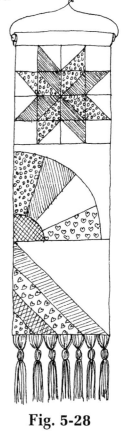

Fig. 5-28

Additional Materials Required

¼ yard each of backing fabric and polyester batting
Bell-pull hardware, available in craft stores
Tassel or fringe trim

Preparation and Construction

1. Sew your finished 4" Quilt blocks together in a row, using ¼" seam allowances.

2. For the bottom of the bell pull, use a ¼" seam allowances to stitch a tassel or fringe trim to one short end, placing face sides and raw edges together.

3. Cut backing fabric and polyester batting equal to the size of your strip of quilt blocks. Lay the backing, face sides together, on the strip of quilt blocks, keeping the fringe or tassel to the inside. Place the polyester batting on top and pin around the edges through all layers.

4. Sew along both long edges and the bottom trimmed edge using a ¼" seam allowance. Clip the corners, and turn it face sides out.

5. Cut a strip of one of the quilt fabrics, 2½" × 4¾". Turn the 2½" sides narrowly to the wrong side with a double-folded hem. Fold this in half lengthwise, with the face side out and raw edges meeting.

6. Insert the raw edges of this strip ¼" into the opening at the top of your bell pull, turning the raw edges of the opening down and in as you do so. Machine topstitch through all layers. To display, insert the bell-pull hardware or a small dowel into the "tube" of fabric created by the strip at the top.

7. Machine quilt following the seam lines of your quilt blocks.

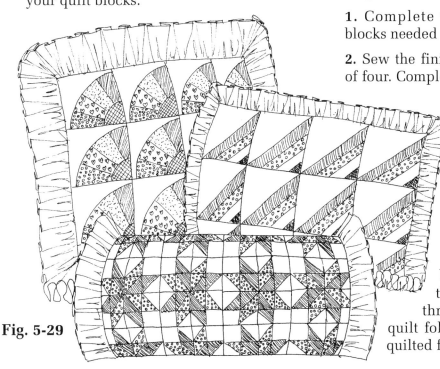

Fig. 5-29

Neck Roll, Boudoir, and Square Pillows

You will need sixteen finished 4" quilt blocks for the square pillow and neck roll (Fig. 5-29). You will need twelve for the boudoir pillow.

Additional Materials Required

Neck Roll: 1¾ yard flat eyelet for ruffle or 1 yard finished ruffle; ⅛ yard extra face fabric; 17" square of backing fabric and of polyester batting for quilting the face of your pillow; neck roll pillow form or extra polyester batting; 1½ yards ⅜"-wide ribbon

Boudoir Pillow: 2 yards flat eyelet trim for ruffle or 1¼ yards finished ruffle; ½ yard backing fabric; polyester batting for quilting the face of your pillow; 12" × 16" pillow form or extra polyester batting

Square Pillow: 3½ yards flat eyelet trim for ruffle or 2 yards finished ruffle; ½ yard backing fabric; polyester batting for quilting the face of your pillow; 16" square pillow form

Preparation and Construction

1. Complete the number of small quilt blocks needed for your project.

2. Sew the finished blocks together in rows of four. Complete the face of each project by sewing the rows together. (Three rows of four blocks for the boudoir pillow, four rows each for the neck roll and square.) Press.

3. Cut backing fabric and polyester batting equal in size to the finished face of your project. Sandwich the polyester batting between the backing and face fabrics, with the fabrics face sides out. Pin through all layers and machine quilt following the seam lines of the quilted face.

To Finish Your Neck Roll

4. Fold your quilted square in half, face sides and raw edges together. Sew along the long edge with a ¼" seam allowance to create a quilted tube. Turn right side out.

5. Stitch a wide basting seam along the raw edge of your flat eyelet and pull the stitches to gather it into a ruffle, *or* use ready-made ruffle. Pin the ruffle, face sides and raw edges together, to the raw edges around the openings at either end of your quilted tube. Sew the ends of the ruffle together with a French seam where they meet. Sew the ruffle to the quilted tube using a ¼" seam allowance.

6. From the extra face fabric, cut two strips 4" × 16½". Fold these in half, face sides together, matching the 4" sides. Sew the 4" sides together on each strip using a ¼" seam allowance, but leave 1½" unsewn at one end of the seam on each piece.

7. Where the seam has been left unsewn, stitch the seam allowance to the wrong side with a straight or zigzag stitch.

8. Fold the raw edge at this end of each piece ¼" to the wrong side, then again ⅝" and press. Cut your ribbon into two pieces, each 27" long. Encase the ribbon inside the folds by straight stitching close to the lower fold. The ends of the ribbon should stick out evenly beyond the seam allowance, and the ribbon should slide back and forth easily within the casing to allow it to be pulled into a tightly gathered circle (Fig. 5-30).

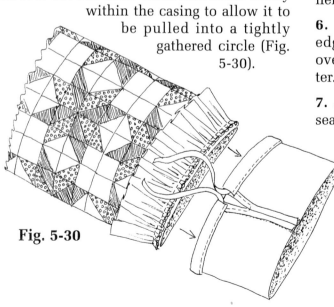

Fig. 5-30

9. Place each of these over the ruffle at either end of your quilted tube, face side in and raw edges matching, and sew in place with a ¼" seam allowance. Serge or zigzag stitch over the raw edges.

10. Pull back the side strips to expose the ruffles and quilted face. At one end, tie the ribbon as tightly as possible to gather it into a tiny circle. Knot the ribbon and tie the ends into a bow.

11. Insert a neck roll pillow form at the other end, and tie it as well. If you can't find a neck roll pillow form, you can roll 17"-wide polyester batting into a tight "jelly roll" and substitute it for the neck roll.

To Finish Your Square or Boudoir Pillow

Follow **Steps 1–3** on page 91.

4. Stitch a wide basting seam along the raw edge of you flat eyelet and pull the stitches to gather it into a ruffle, *or* use ready-made ruffle. Pin the ruffle, face sides and raw edges together, around the edges of your quilted pillow face. Using a French seam, sew the ends of the ruffle together where they meet. Sew the ruffle to the pillow face with a ¼" seam allowance.

5. Cut two pieces of backing fabric, 10" × 17" for the square pillow, and 10" × 13" for the boudoir pillow. Hem a 17" or a 13" edge on each piece with a narrow, double-folded hem.

6. Place the backing face sides and raw edges together on the ruffled pillow face, overlapping the hemmed edges in the center. Pin around all sides to hold.

7. Sew the backing to the face with a ¼" seam allowance. Serge or zigzag around the raw edges. Turn your pillow right side out through the overlapped backing. Insert a purchased pillow form or folded polyester batting to fit.

Bibliography

Brown, Gail. *Instant Interiors.* Menlo Park, CA: Open Chain Publishing, 1992.

——. *Gail Brown's All New Instant Interiors.* Radnor, PA: Chilton Book Company, 1992.

Colvin, Maggie. *Pure Fabrication.* Radnor, PA: Chilton Book Company, 1985.

Fanning, Robbie and Tony. *Complete Book of Machine Quilting.* Radnor, PA: Chilton Book Company, 1980.

Hargrave, Harriet. *Mastering Machine Appliqué.* Lafayette, CA: C & T Publishing, 1991.

Hinson, Delores. *A Quilter's Companion.* New York: Arco Publishing, Inc., 1984.

Johannah, Barbara. *The Quick Quiltmaking Handbook.* Self-published, 1988.

——. *Crystal Piecing.* Radnor, PA: Chilton Book Company, 1993.

And for more easy quilting projects:

Eaton, Kathleen. *Super Simple Quilts.* Radnor, PA: Chilton Book Company, 1992.

Jacobson, Anthony and Jeanne. *Quilting Around Your Home.* Radnor, PA: Chilton Book Company, 1993.

Resource List

Nancy's Notions, Ltd., a sewing supply catalog and retail store. 333 Biecl Ave., P.O. Box 683, Beaver Dam, WI 53916. (800-833-0690)

Keepsake Quilting, a specialty quilting supply catalog. Dover Street, P.O. Box 1459, Meredith, NH 03253.

ADJ Designs (No-Sew Window Shade kits) 435 Meadow Lane, Carlstadt, NJ 07072.

Morning Glory Products, quality batting and fiberfill. P.O. Box 979, Taylor, TX 76574. (Write for information on where to find these products near you.)

Index